# Sexuality and the Person with Traumatic Brain Injury

A Guide for Families

# Sexuality and the Person with Traumatic Brain Injury
## A Guide for Families

**Ernest R Griffith, MD**
>*Currently*, Private Practice
>Physical Medicine and Rehabilitation
>Phoenix, Arizona
>and
>Medical Director, Brain Injury Continuum
>Meridian Point Rehabilitation Hospital and Scottsdale
>Community Services
>Scottsdale, Arizona
>
>*Formerly*, Professor and Head
>Department of Physical Medicine and Rehabilitation
>University of Illinois at Chicago College of Medicine
>Chicago, Illinois

**Sally Lemberg, MSW, ACSW**
>*Currently*, Clinical Social Worker
>and
>Board Certified Diplomate
>Mesa, Arizona
>
>*Formerly*, President
>Arizona Head Injury Foundation
>and
>Member
>Governor's Task Force on Head Injury

 F. A. DAVIS COMPANY • Philadelphia

Printed in the United States of America

Last digit indicates print number:  10  9  8  7  6  5  4  3  2  1

senior allied health editor:   Jean-François Vilain
senior allied health development editor:   Ralph Zickgraf
production editor:   Gail Shapiro
designer:   Donald B. Freggens, Jr.

As new scientific information becomes available through basic and clinical research, recommended treatments and drug therapies undergo changes. The author(s) and publisher have done everything possible to make this book accurate, up to date, and in accord with accepted standards at the time of publication. The authors, editors, and publisher are not responsible for errors or omissions or for consequences from application of the book, and make no warranty, expressed or implied, in regard to the contents of the book. Any practice described in this book should be applied by the reader in accordance with professional standards of care used in regard to the unique circumstances that may apply in each situation. The reader is advised always to check product information (package inserts) for changes and new information regarding dose and contraindications before administering any drug. Caution is especially urged when using new or infrequently ordered drugs.

**Library of Congress Cataloging-in-Publication Data**

Griffith, Ernest R., 1949-
    Sexuality and the person with traumatic brain injury : a guide for
families / Ernest R. Griffith, Sally Lemberg.
        p.   cm.
    Includes bibliographical references and index.
    ISBN 0-8036-4408-6 (acid-free) :
    1. Brain damage—Patients—Sexual behavior.   2. Sexual disorders—
Treatment.   I. Lemberg, Sally, 1951-   .   II. Title.
RC387.5.G75   1992
616.85'83—dc20                                                          92-32994
                                                                              CIP

Authorization to photocopy items for internal or personal use, or the internal or personal use of specific clients, is granted by F.A. Davis Company for users registered with the Copyright Clearance Center (CCC) Transactional Reporting Service, provided that the fee of $.10 per copy is paid directly to CCC, 27 Congress St., Salem, MA 01970. For those organizations that have been granted a photocopy license by CCC, a separate system of payment has been arranged. The fee code for users of the Transactional Reporting Service is: 8036-4408/92 0 + $.10.

To the Memory of Doctor Shelly Berroll

*intrepid pioneer in brain injury rehabilitation, esteemed teacher and physician, tireless ambassador, wise counselor, joyous celebrant of life, and beloved pal.*

*To persons with brain injury and their families.*

# PREFACE

This book is an attempt to share with families current information on sexuality and sexual function of the brain-injured person. The subject has not received much attention in the medical literature until quite recently. There is still much that we do not know, but the future looks promising. Much needed research is underway in several head injury centers. The fruits of these investigations are already evident. A June 1990 volume of the *Journal of Traumatic Brain Injury* is devoted entirely to the subject of sexuality. Some of the articles of that volume detail the outcomes of fresh clinical research.

Advances in methods of assessment and treatment of sexual function are being applied to brain-injured people. In these regards we have more to offer than at any previous time. The resources and services for persons with brain injury and their families have grown appreciably in recent years. We have identified a number of these resources at the end of the book. The National Head Injury Foundation has been the leading national advocate for people with brain injury and their families. We are pleased to have had their support on this project.

We hope that this book will add to the understanding that all of us are sexual beings—however that sexuality may be felt or expressed. We hope that the book conveys that a person's sexuality is vulnerable to the many physical, psychological, and social consequences of brain injury. We are confident that much more can be done to restore sexual health and function to those brain-injured persons who have experienced change in their sexual lives.

A glossary of terms is included at the end of the book.

For the interested reader, the terms and their definitions are arranged according to consecutive reference numbers that appear after the related words or phrases in the text. The terms are also listed alphabetically, followed by their reference numbers. A reading list is also appended to the book.

Our special thanks to Brenda Thomas and Cherie Lane, who typed the manuscript, and to Jean-François Vilain and Ralph Zickgraf, our persevering editors.

*Ernest R. Griffith*
*Sally Lemberg*

# CONTENTS

# Introduction

This book is intended to be a resource to the partner and family of the person with traumatic brain injury[1] (TBI). It provides current information on sexuality, describes the principles of dealing with problems and concerns regarding sexuality, and offers further sources of information and assistance.

Human sexuality is the sum of all those biological and psychological factors relating to our capacity to love, to be loved, and to reproduce. Biological factors include such aspects as whether we are male or female, our basic sex drive, and sexual responses. These responses are:

1. *Sexual arousal* or *excitement*: erection of the penis or clitoris, and vaginal lubrication; associated reactions are breast engorgement, skin flush, and increased sexual desire.
2. *Plateau*: heightening of reactions of excitement; can lead to orgasm with sufficient stimulation.
3. *Orgasm*: "coming" or reaching a climax; in the male, normally associated with expression of semen (ejaculation).[2]
4. *Resolution*: returning of the sex organs to the prearousal state.

Fertility and childbearing capabilities are additional biological aspects of sexuality. Psychological factors include sexual beliefs, attitudes, and interests; sexual behaviors and practices; feelings of caring, loving, and intimacy; and appreciating our sexual identity and feeling comfortable with it. Sexuality is made up of all of these factors, and is an evolving and changing process from conception throughout life.

Far transcending sexual activities, sexuality also concerns the view of ourselves and others as attractive, loving, and lovable persons. Our manly and womanly characteristics—our manner of talking, walking, grooming, dressing, and behaving—are daily expressions of sexuality. Hence, sexuality is an integral part of our physical, mental, and social wholeness. Disease or disability often affects our sexuality. Therefore, sexuality is a vital health issue and deserves the same attention and care as other life functions. Why then has sexuality not received full recognition as a major health concern?

In the past, health professionals, including physicians, have not been adequately educated and trained in human sexuality. Fortunately this deficiency has improved, to a large extent, in the past 15 years. Both professionals and the public have been uncomfortable in fully exploring sexual functioning as a routine part of health assessment because the subject is an intimate and sensitive one. All of us have been exposed to its many myths and taboos. Many of us experience insecurities in dealing with our own sexuality. Thus there has been a reluctance to fully and frankly discuss it. We are witnessing the progressive erosion of these old barriers, an era of fuller interest and attention to the subject, and a time of discoveries in the realm of diagnosis and treatment that afford fresh optimism in dealing with sexual problems.

With an estimated incidence of over 1 million new injuries per year in the United States, TBI is an immense health problem. Since the majority of those injured do not die, the number of survivors, many with remaining deficits, is growing annually. The survivors are predominantly young people entering or already at the peak of sexual interest and activity. It is fair to estimate that nearly all of these survivors, at one time or another, have some disturbances of sexual function. Until very recently, it was believed that most sexual dysfunctions[3] following brain injury were the result of psychological and social problems relating to mental deficits associated with the injury, as well as reactions of the person, family, and community to the physical, mental, and social consequences of the injury. That belief is currently being re-examined in light of new research and clinical information. While not discounting the influence of psychosocial factors, we find that biological factors account for dysfunction more frequently than previously thought.

# Basics of Normal Sexual Development, Anatomy, and Function

Puberty is the time of sexual awakening and development. Starting at about age 9 to 10 years, girls begin to grow pubic hair, experience enlargement of their nipples and breasts, and begin to have menstrual periods. They grow rapidly in height and weight, and assume the characteristic wide pelvis and body build of young women. Ovulation begins, sometimes before periods become regular. Most girls become self-conscious and worry about how they look and how attractive they are to others.

Boys usually begin puberty a year or two later than girls. They too develop pubic hair and grow rapidly. Their muscles develop and strengthen. They grow facial hair and their voices lower in pitch. Like girls, boys experience enlargement and increased sensitivity of their genital organs and grow hair in their armpits. Boys have erections very readily, even by just thinking about a desirable person. They begin to ''come'' or ''shoot,'' that is, expel seminal fluid[4] from the penis when they masturbate to the point of orgasm.[5] Some fluid may seep out before orgasm or without orgasm. If this seepage happens during intercourse, pregnancy may result. During sleep, erections occur repeatedly. These erections often are associated with dreams. Sometimes these erections result in the expelling of seminal fluid and the sensation of orgasm (nocturnal emissions[6] or "wet dreams"). Boys, like girls, become concerned about their bodies, their physical skills, and their attractiveness. Acne may become a problem with either sex.

Actually, we are sexually responsive from infancy onward. Infants and toddlers are curious adventurers, exploring their own genital organs as well as those of others. Local stimulation of the genitalia,[7] even the rubbing of tight clothing, can produce erections of the penis or engorgement of the girl's labia and clitoris. Before puberty, children are capable of having the same types of sexual responses as adults: arousal, plateau, orgasm, and resolution. However, the child's responses are less intense and less likely to proceed to orgasm.

The adult female external genital organs are illustrated in Figure 1. The labia minora[8] (smaller lips) and clitoris become engorged with sexual arousal. The clitoris[9] is much like a miniature penis. Many women require sustained stimulation of the clitoris in order to have orgasm. Proper positioning during intercourse can produce effective clitoral stimulation. Other methods may include application of an electric vibrator, gentle rubbing with a finger, and oral stimulation.

The virgin may have an intact hymen, a membrane encircling the entrance of the vagina. The hymen sometimes tears and bleeds during the first penetration. However, with adequate lubrication and gentle penetration, the hymen may stretch without discomfort.

During arousal, the vagina secretes a mucous liquid that serves as a lubricant to ease penetration. Along with the engorgement of the genital organs and breasts, the presence of this fluid indicates that the woman is sexually aroused. The female urethra, the passage conducting urine from the bladder to the exterior, is separate from the clitoris. (The male urethra passes through the penis.) The opening of the

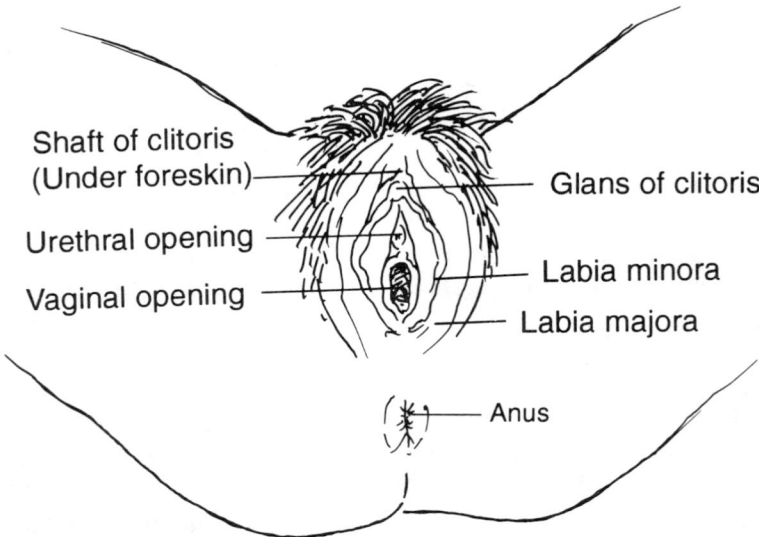

**Figure 1.** The female external genital organs. (From Scanlon, VC and Sanders, T: Essentials of Anatomy and Physiology. FA Davis, Philadelphia, 1991, p 471, with permission.)

female urethra is located between the clitoris and the vagina. The position and the short length of the woman's urethra make her susceptible to bladder infections, especially after repeated and vigorous sexual activity. The woman can reduce the risk of such infections by emptying the bladder immediately after sexual activity.

The female internal genital organs are the ovaries,[10] the fallopian tubes,[11] and the uterus[12] (womb) (Fig. 2). The two ovaries produce most of the female hormones. These hormones stimulate the changes of puberty, regulate the periods and the production of eggs (ova), and maintain the structure and function of the sexual organs. Along with their other functions, the hormones maintain the secondary sexual characteristics: distribution of body fat, shape of the pelvis, freedom from facial hair, and so forth. Typically, nearly every month from puberty until menopause, either ovary generates a mature egg that erupts from the surface of the ovary, enters one of the fallopian tubes, and travels through the tube until it reaches the womb. If fertilization of the egg occurs, it normally takes place in the tube. The fertilized egg then proceeds to implant itself in the inner lining of the uterus.

The male external genital organs are shown in Figure 3.

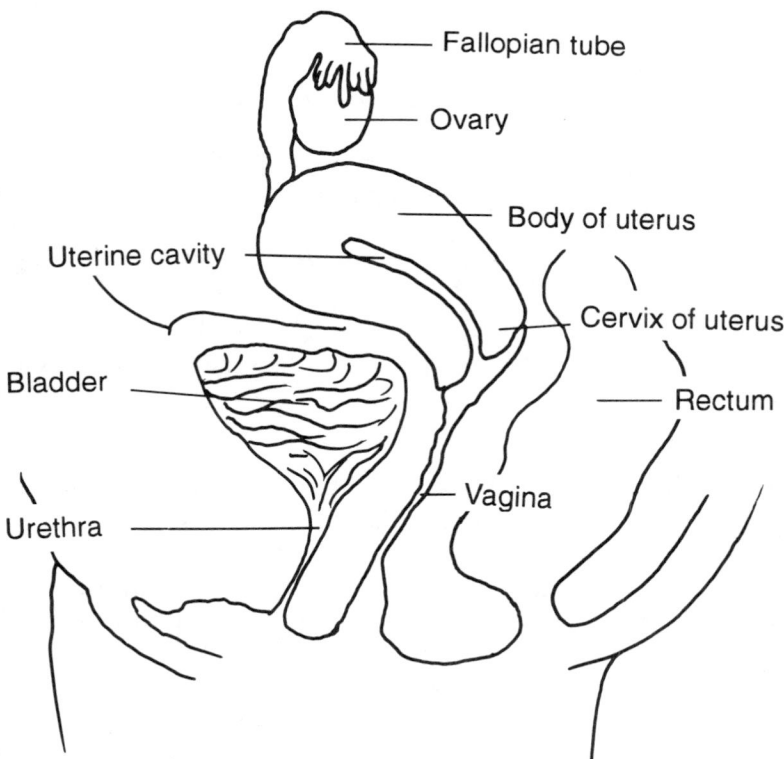

**Figure 2.** Female internal genital organs. (From Scanlon, VC and Sanders, T: Essentials of Anatomy and Physiology. FA Davis, Philadelphia, 1991, p 466, with permission.)

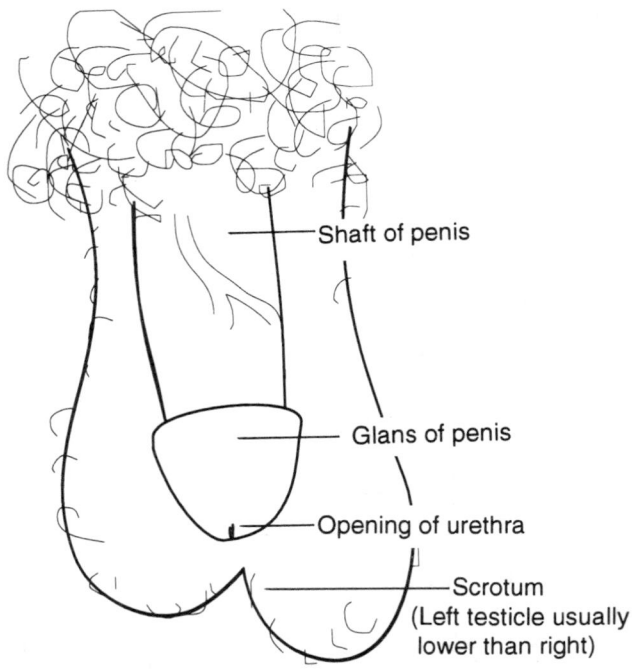

Shaft of penis

Glans of penis

Opening of urethra

Scrotum
(Left testicle usually
lower than right)

**Figure 3.** The male external genital organs (circumcised penis).

The penis, like the clitoris, consists of a shaft and a tip or glans. The glans of the penis, like that of the clitoris, is covered by a hood of skin (the foreskin) that retracts during erection. In man, the foreskin is often surgically removed. This surgical removal is called circumcision. The man who has not been circumcised should regularly retract the foreskin so that its oily secretions, smegma, can be cleaned from the penis. The glans of either the penis or the clitoris is usually very sensitive and may be irritated by rough stimulation. The shaft of either organ consists of tissue which is extremely rich in blood vessels, allowing engorgement and erection upon stimulation.

The scrotum is the sack containing a testicle[13] on each side. It also contains a smaller attachment, the epididymis,[14] and two tubes, the vas deferens[15] (Fig. 4). The two testicles are the site where most of the male hormones are made. The male hormones stimulate the changes of puberty and maintain the structure and function of the male sex organs. Furthermore, the hormones regulate the formation of spermatozoa[16] and the secretions that nourish the cells. In addition, the male hormones maintain the secondary sexual characteristics such as beard growth, hairy body, muscular development, low-pitched voice, and so forth.

Once the sperm cells have matured in the testicle, they are stored in the epididymis. With orgasm, the sperm and seminal fluid are propelled through the tubes into the upper end of the urethra. Along the way, further secretions are added by glands, including the seminal vesicles[17] and the prostate gland.[18]

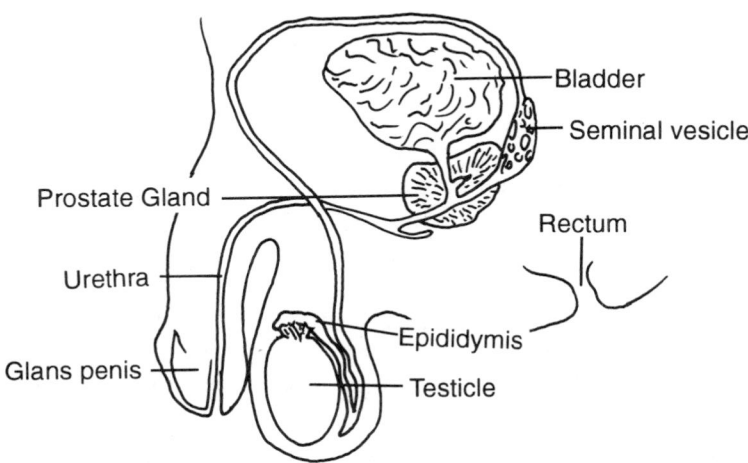

**Figure 4.** Male internal genital organs, side view. (From Scanlon, VC and Sanders, T: Essentials of Anatomy and Physiology. FA Davis, Philadelphia, 1991, p 462, with permission.)

With ejaculation, the muscle surrounding the bladder outlet to the urethra shuts off the outlet so that urine does not enter the urethra and seminal fluid cannot escape into the bladder. The fluid is expelled through the urethra and out the opening at the end of the penis.

With penile-vaginal intercourse, the seminal fluid enters the vagina and is propelled into the uterus through an opening in the neck of the womb. The sperm cells continue their journey through the uterine cavity, entering the fallopian tubes, where fertilization of the egg occurs. The neck of the womb, the cervix, can be touched at the end of the vagina by the penis or the examining finger. In the nonpregnant state, the cervix feels firm with a consistency like that of the tip of the nose. Vigorous manipulation of the cervix may cause some women pelvic discomfort.

The full cycle of sexual responses of men and women includes the four phases of excitement, plateau, orgasm, and resolution (Tables 1 and 2). Although these phases are very similar for both sexes, there are some differences that merit attention.

The excitement phase is often more rapidly attained in men. Full penile erection can occur within a few seconds. Either sex can be inhibited from sexual excitement or lose engorgement by sudden distractions or uncomfortable physical or emotional stimuli such as pain or anxiety. Frequently, men progress more rapidly than women through the phases of excitement and plateau to orgasm. This situation can leave a female partner at a stage of excitement or plateau, unless she is further stimulated effectively. In that event, one of several methods can be used to reduce the man's speed of progress and allow his partner to reach orgasm before he does. The female orgasm may be abruptly terminated by a disturbance, whereas the male orgasm ordinarily is not interrupted once ejaculation of semen begins.

Immediately following orgasm, the male resolution phase is marked by a variable period of time, usually several

**Table 1**

## SEXUAL RESPONSE CYCLE: GENERAL BODY REACTIONS

### Excitement

Nipple erection
    Women—Routinely
    Men—30%
Skin flush
    Women—25%

### Plateau

Skin flush
    Women—75%
    Men—25%
Increased muscle tension
Rapid, deep breathing
Rapid heart beat
Rise in blood pressure

### Orgasm

Facial and pelvic muscle contractions
Rapid, deep breathing
Rapid heart beat
Rise in blood pressure

### Resolution

Sweating (40% of both sexes)
Rapid, deep breathing
Rapid heart rate subsiding
Blood pressure dropping
Muscle relaxation

---

minutes, when any stimulus will generally be ineffective in producing an erection. This is called the refractory period. The refractory period of younger males may allow delayed or partial erections to occur with strong stimulation.

**Table 2**

## SEXUAL RESPONSE CYCLE: GENITAL ORGAN REACTIONS

| *Female* | *Male* |
| --- | --- |
| **Excitement** | |
| Vaginal lubrication | Erection of penis |
| Engorgement of vaginal walls, labia minor, and clitoris | Elevation of scrotum |
| Flattening of labia major | Elevation and engorgement of testicles |
| Increased vaginal capacity as uterus elevates | |
| Breast engorgement | |
| **Plateau (Further Increases in Reactions of Excitement)** | |
| Discoloration of labia minor<br>  Red if no previous deliveries<br>  Purple if previous deliveries | Purple discoloration of glans penis |
| | Small emissions of seminal fluid |
| **Orgasm** | |
| Contractions of muscles of uterus and pelvic floor | Contraction of muscles of glands contributing to seminal fluid and of urethral and pelvic floor muscles |
| **Resolution** | |
| Gradual loss of pelvic congestion and engorgement | Refractory period with rapid loss of pelvic congestion and engorgement |
| Loss of breast engorgement | Loss of erection |
| Loss of discoloration of labia minor | |

The female phase of resolution does not have this early refractory period. Therefore, with continued stimulation, the woman may almost immediately proceed to another orgasm.

With either sex, the length of the resolution phase is related to the length of the preceding phases. Resolution may last many hours if excitement and plateau have been slow to develop. Prolonged excitement and plateau without orgasm can result in extreme congestion of the genital organs during resolution, producing pain and tenderness of the organs, particularly the testicles ("blue balls") or ovaries. Masturbation to orgasm helps to relieve this uncomfortable state.

# Brain Anatomy and Function

A basic understanding of the structures of the brain,[19] as well as their functions, is helpful in appreciating what areas of the brain are prone to injury. This understanding also aids in appreciating how injuries to brain structure can result in disabilities relating to sexual functions.

Let us look at that remarkable structure within our skulls: the brain. It consists of a mass of delicate soft tissue that when viewed from the side looks much like a boxing glove (Fig. 5). The brain is covered by three layers of membrane called the *meninges*.

The largest part of the brain, the *cerebrum*,[20] is the center for higher mental and motor activities. The cerebrum is divided into two halves, the left and right *cerebral hemispheres*[20] (Figs. 6 and 7), by a cleft (fissure). The left cerebral hemisphere is the *dominant* hemisphere for over 90 percent of us. By dominant, we mean that the major centers for speech, writing, and reading are located on that side. Most left-hemisphere-dominant people are right-handed. Only about 7 percent of us have a right-hemisphere-dominant brain. A majority of this group is left-handed. In any case, the dominant hemisphere is our reasoning, analytical, scientific, language, and symbol-oriented brain. The opposite, or *nondominant*, side is our creative, artistic, emotional, intuitive, "see things as a whole," brain. These two brains really work as one. They are connected together by multiple pathways. The *corpus callosum*[21] (Fig. 8) is a major connection between the hemispheres. It is a body of densely packed nerve fibers (white matter) lying deep within the cerebrum. Each cerebral hemisphere is further divided by fissures into four lobes.

As the name indicates, the *frontal lobe*[22] occupies the front of the hemisphere (Fig. 9). The frontal lobe is the seat of expressive speech in the dominant hemisphere (Fig. 10). At the back of the lobe is the *motor strip*, the site of control of movements on the opposite side of the body. In front of the motor strip lies the *prefrontal area*[23] of the lobe. This area is the seat of personality and planning.

The *parietal lobe*[24] is situated behind the frontal lobe (Fig. 11). Along its front border lies the *sensory strip* (Fig. 10). The

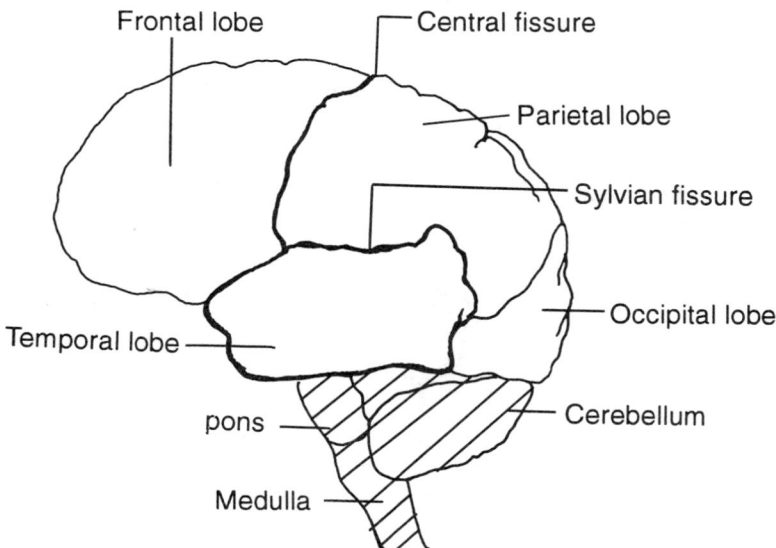

**Figure 5.** Left side of the brain, showing the four lobes of the cerebrum and most of the brain stem (*shaded*).

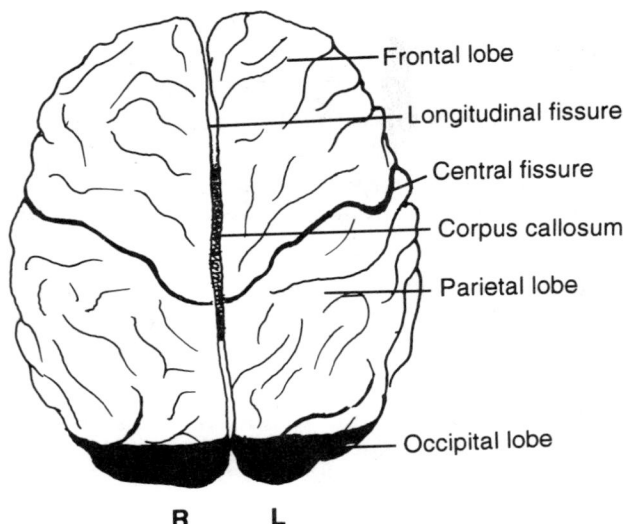

**Figure 6.** View of brain from above, showing left (L) and right (R) cerebral hemispheres.

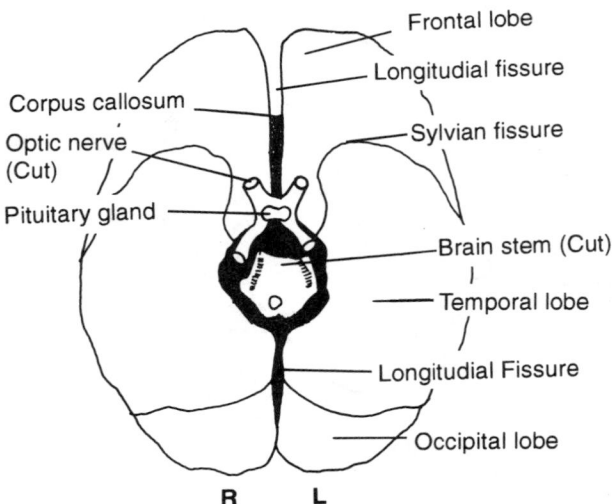

**Figure 7.** View of brain from below, showing right (R) and left (L) cerebral hemispheres.

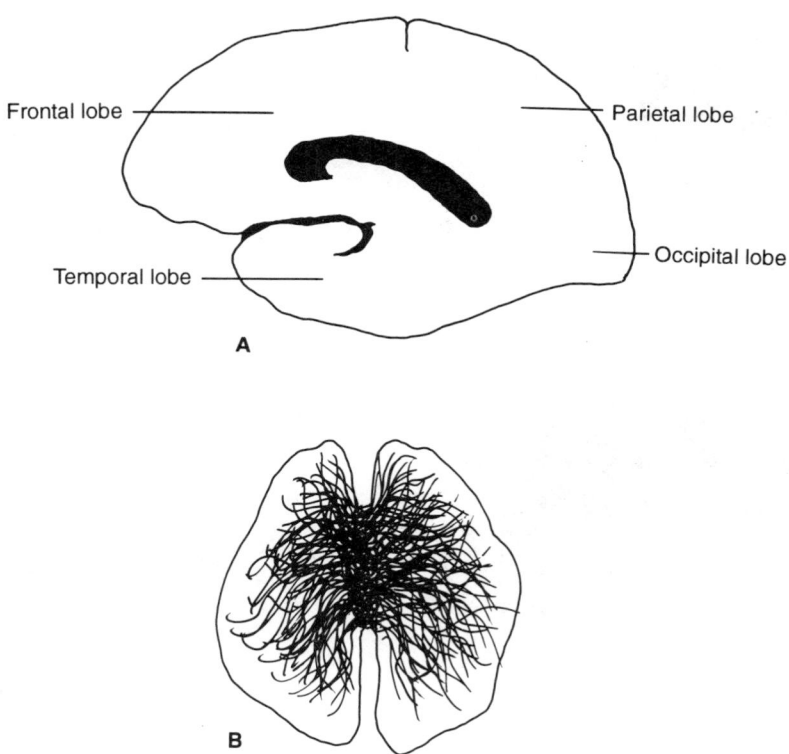

**Figure 8.** The corpus callosum. (A) The inner surface of the right cerebral hemisphere, with the corpus callosum (*shaded*). (B) View of brain from above, showing the corpus callosum and its connections with the cerebral hemispheres.

sensory strip is the highest center of interpretation of sensations coming from the opposite side of the body: touch, pressure, pain, temperature, position sense, and vibration. These sensory interpretations are integrated with past and present experiences and future plans or expectations. That integrative process is termed *perception*.

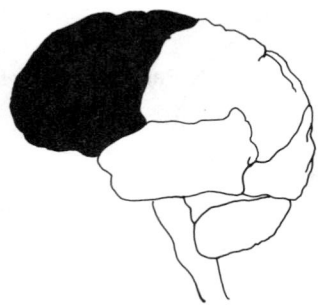

**A    LEFT SIDE OF BRAIN**

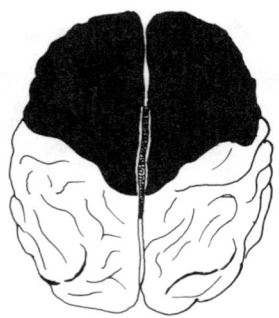

**B    VIEW FROM ABOVE**

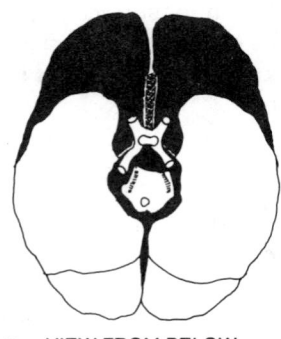

**C    VIEW FROM BELOW**

**Figure 9.** The frontal lobes (*shaded*), viewed from (A) left, (B) above, and (C) below.

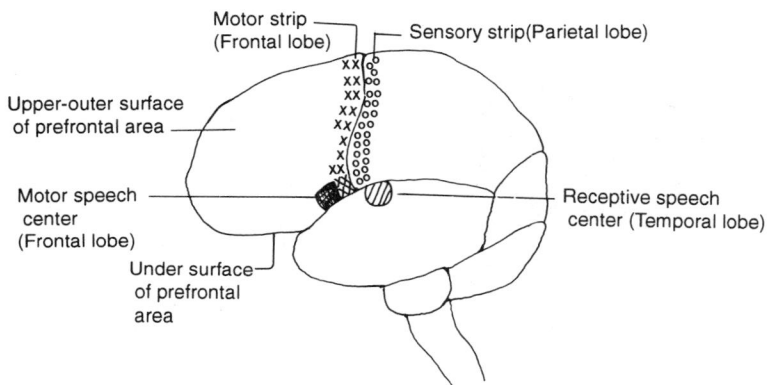

**Figure 10.** Some of the functional areas of the cerebral lobes (seen from the left). The motor strip, at the rear of the left frontal lobe, controls movements on the right side of the body. The sensory strip, at the front of the left parietal lobe, processes and interprets sensations from the right side of the body.

Beneath the parietal lobe projects the "thumb of the boxing glove," the *temporal lobe*[25] (Fig. 12). The centers of taste, smell, hearing, learning, and language understanding are located here. The *limbic system*[26] is an extension of the temporal lobe that adjoins deeper structures to form a ring of connecting groups of cell bodies (Fig. 13). The limbic system is the source of memory, emotional aspects of sensory experiences, and bodily urges, including sex drive.

The *occipital lobe*[27] is located behind the parietal lobe in the back of the cerebrum (Fig. 14). It is the primary center of vision. A summary of important functions of the four lobes is presented in Figure 15.

The cerebral hemispheres are covered by a layer of *gray matter*,[28] mainly nerve cells, called the *cerebral cortex*.[29] Under the cortex is the *white matter*,[30] nerve fibers that connect nerve cells together. The white matter sometimes connects cells

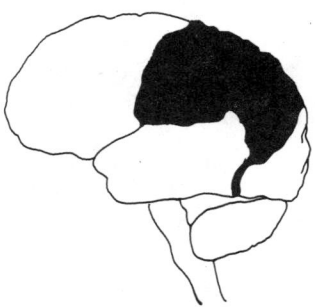

**A**   LEFT SIDE OF BRAIN

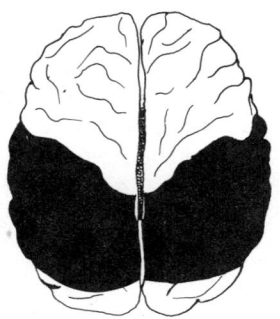

**B**   VIEW FROM ABOVE

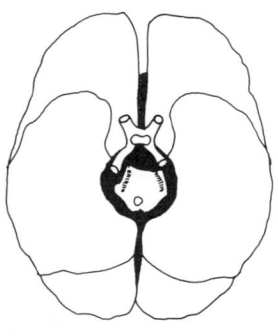

**C**   VIEW FROM BELOW

**Figure 11.** The parietal lobes (*shaded*), viewed from (A) left, (B) above, and (C) below.

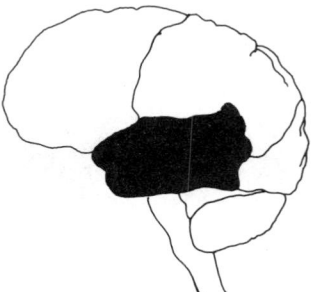

**A**   LEFT SIDE OF BRAIN

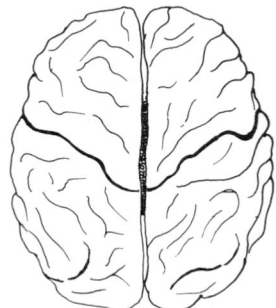

**B**   VIEW FROM ABOVE

**Figure 12.** The temporal lobes (*shaded*), viewed from (A) left, (B) above, and (C) below.

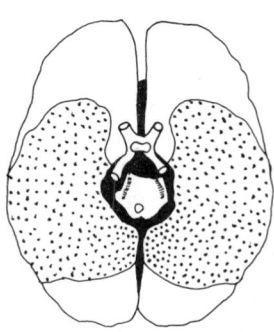

**C**   VIEW FROM BELOW

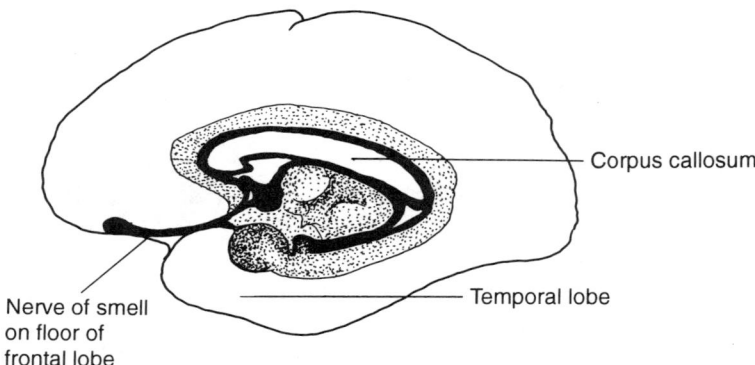

Corpus callosum

Nerve of smell
on floor of
frontal lobe

Temporal lobe

**Figure 13.** The inner surface of the right cerebral hemisphere showing the ring of limbic system structures around the corpus callosum.

that are close together and sometimes connects cells that are far apart. Also, deep within each hemisphere is a fluid-filled cavity, the *lateral ventricle*.[31] The ventricles are part of a system that makes cerebrospinal fluid[32] and distributes it to various parts of the brain and spinal cord. The pressure of the fluid, *intracranial pressure*,[33] is one indicator of the severity of brain injury and the response to treatment.

The cerebral hemispheres cover a smaller area of the brain known as the *diencephalon*.[34] Several closely related groups of nerve cells are located here. The *basal ganglia*[35] are located on each side of the two lateral ventricles. These centers govern initiation of movement and regulate posture.

We have already mentioned the *limbic system*. That system has many connections with the *hypothalamus*,[36] a center that regulates blood pressure, heart rate, and breathing, as well as basic drives and emotions. The hypothalamus, in turn, is connected to the *pituitary gland*[37] (Fig. 16), the "master gland," which is the size and shape of a pea. The pituitary gland produces hormones: chemicals that travel in the

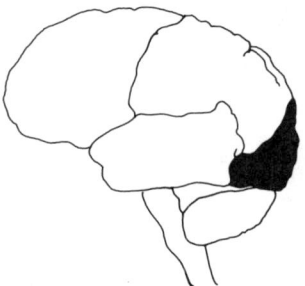

**A    LEFT SIDE OF BRAIN**

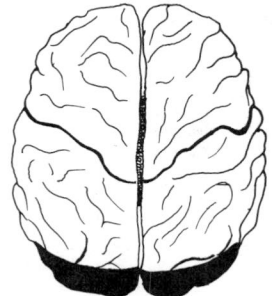

**B    VIEW FROM ABOVE**

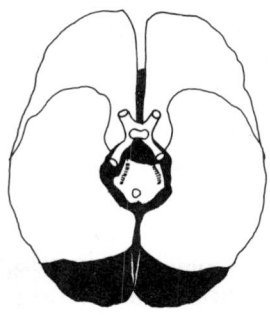

**Figure 14.** The occipital lobes (*shaded*), viewed from (A) left, (B) above, and (C) below.

**C    VIEW FROM BELOW**

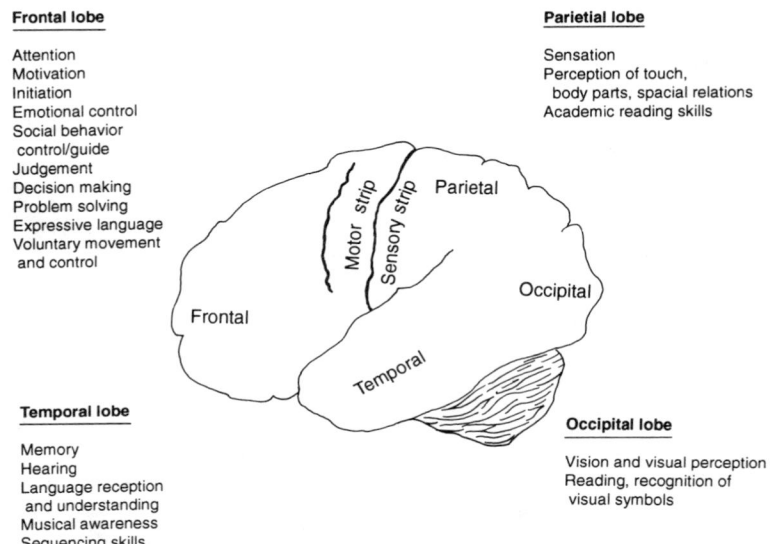

**Frontal lobe**

Attention
Motivation
Initiation
Emotional control
Social behavior
 control/guide
Judgement
Decision making
Problem solving
Expressive language
Voluntary movement
 and control

**Parietal lobe**

Sensation
Perception of touch,
 body parts, spacial relations
Academic reading skills

**Temporal lobe**

Memory
Hearing
Language reception
 and understanding
Musical awareness
Sequencing skills

**Occipital lobe**

Vision and visual perception
Reading, recognition of
 visual symbols

**Figure 15.** Certain functions are associated with each of the four lobes of the brain.

bloodstream to regulate vital glands such as the ovaries, the testicles, the adrenals, and the thyroid. The pituitary gland also regulates body water through its action on the kidneys.

The *thalamus*[38] (Fig. 16) is a major relay station for all kinds of sensory information coming from the head and body, much of it on its way to the parietal lobe.

Immediately below the thalamus, and connected to the diencephalon, is the *brainstem*[39] (Fig. 16). It consists of three parts: *midbrain*,[40] *pons*,[41] and *medulla*.[42] The *cerebellum*[43] lies behind the brainstem and is connected to the pons. It looks like a miniature cerebrum.

The brainstem houses most of the *cranial nerves*[44] (Table 3) (some of which receive information from the skin and mus-

**Table 3**

## TWELVE PAIRS OF CRANIAL NERVES (RIGHT AND LEFT)

| Number | Name | Function |
|--------|------|----------|
| 1 | Optic nerve | Vision |
| 2 | Olfactory nerve | Smell |
| 3 | Oculomotor nerve | Eye movement<br>Regulation of pupils and lenses |
| 4 | Trochlear nerve | Eye movement |
| 5 | Trigeminal nerve | Jaw muscles<br>Sensation of face and mucous membranes of eye, nose, and mouth |
| 6 | Abducens nerve | Eye movement |
| 7 | Facial nerve | Facial muscles<br>Taste<br>Tear production<br>Saliva production |
| 8 | Acoustic nerve | Hearing<br>Equilibrium<br>Head and neck position and movement |
| 9 | Glossopharyngeal nerve | Muscles of swallowing<br>Taste<br>Sensation of throat<br>Saliva production |
| 10 | Vagal nerve | Muscles of swallowing<br>Muscles of voice production<br>Regulation of internal organs such as heart, lungs, and gastrointestinal tract |
| 11 | Accessory nerve | Two muscles of neck and shoulder blade |
| 12 | Hypoglossal nerve | Muscles of tongue |

cles of the head) and the special sensory organs of hearing, taste, and balance. Other cranial nerves control the muscles of the face, neck, and eyes. The *reticular activating system*[45] is located throughout the brainstem. It regulates the states of sleep, arousal, and wakefulness. The cerebellum coordinates posture and movement. Centers for blood pressure and breathing control are located in the medulla. The brainstem transmits major connecting circuits between the spinal cord and the higher brain centers.

The *spinal cord*[46] lies below the brainstem (Fig. 16). It sends sensory information from skin, joints, and muscles of the trunk and limbs to the brainstem, diencephalon, and cerebrum. It also transmits information from the higher centers, as well as from its own nerve cells, out to the trunk and

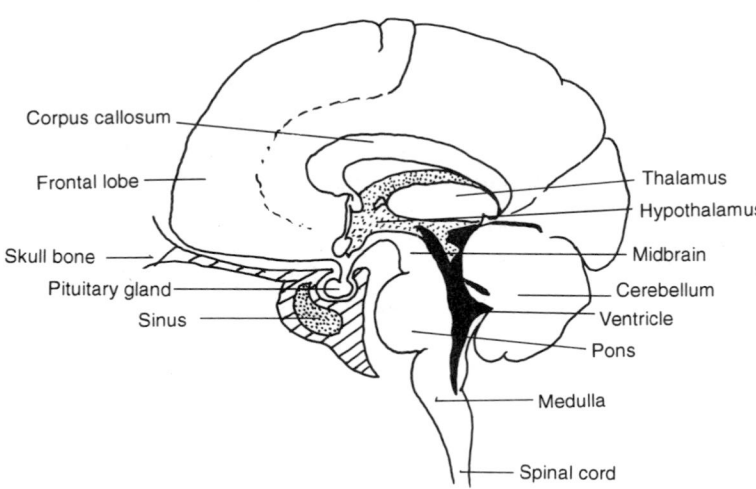

**Figure 16.** Cross-section of the brain, showing right cerebral hemisphere and brainstem. (From Scanlon, VC and Sanders, T: Essentials of Anatomy and Physiology, FA Davis, Philadelphia, 1991, p 174, with permission.)

limb muscles to command reflex and voluntary movements and postures.

The brain, brainstem, and spinal cord together are termed the *central nervous system*.

We will look more closely at many of these structures to see how their altered function after brain injury can affect sexuality.

# Types of Brain Injury

## DEFINITION AND MECHANISMS OF INJURY

What is traumatic brain injury? We can define it as any form of mechanical damage to the brain. Although encased in the protective bony skull, the softer substance of the brain is vulnerable to severe or repeated blows to the head that may not necessarily break the skull. Any object that pierces the skull—a bullet, shell fragment, or other foreign material—may penetrate the brain. Extreme jolts or twists of the brain, such as with the sudden stop of a high speed vehicle collision, can cause brain injury without a direct blow. Such jolts or twists may force prominences of the brain, especially the frontal and temporal poles (Fig. 17), against inner projections of the skull, producing injury. In the United States the most common cause of traumatic brain injury is motor vehicle accidents.

## DIFFUSE PLUS FOCAL INJURIES

Usually the more severe brain injuries resulting from vehicular accidents are diffuse,[47] involving widespread areas of cerebrum and brainstem. The white matter is particularly prone to injury in high speed collisions; often the nerve fibers of the corpus callosum and the midbrain are disrupted. As a result, coma may last for days or weeks. In addition to the diffuse injuries, localized (focal) areas of injury may be

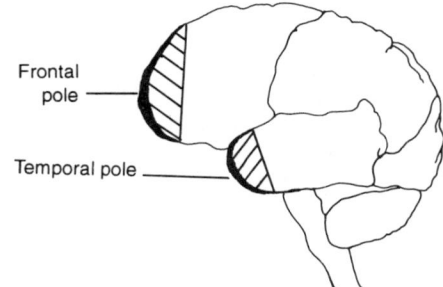

Frontal pole

Temporal pole

**A** LEFT SIDE OF BRAIN

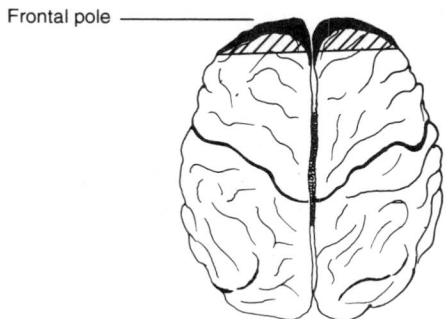

Frontal pole

**B** VIEW FROM ABOVE

**Figure 17.** The poles (*dark shading*) of the temporal and frontal lobes, viewed from (A) left, (B) above, and (C) below. These areas of the brain are vulnerable to damage from extreme jolts or twists that slam the brain against the inner surface of the skull.

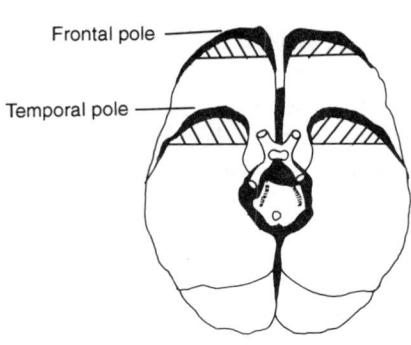

Frontal pole

Temporal pole

**C** VIEW FROM BELOW

present. The frontal and/or temporal poles are often bruised or crushed, frequently on both sides.

Bleeding of the brain's surface or interior may compress surrounding or distant brain tissue. The bleeding may be extensive or expand in size causing extreme swelling, increased internal pressure, blood vessel spasm, and anoxia[48] to the brain. These secondary changes can add to the original diffuse injuries and further threaten life. Large areas of bleeding and crushed, dead brain tissue are surgically removed whenever possible in order to prevent or alleviate these secondary complications. Diffuse injuries may cause disruption of key areas of white matter in parts of the cerebral hemispheres and brainstem. This type of injury is not visible to the naked eye or on x-ray (computerized tomography of the brain; CT scan).[49] However, it is a serious type of injury, often producing extended periods of coma.

Local injuries such as lacerations, bruises, and small, multiple sites of bleeding may be seen in one or more areas of the brain along with diffuse injuries.

Diffuse injuries frequently involve deep hemisphere and diencephalic structures that regulate sexual function. Severe head injuries can directly injure the pituitary gland, which regulates the ovaries and testes. Injuries to the nearby hypothalamus also can disturb pituitary gland function and cause deficiencies in function of the ovaries and testes.

In addition, damage to the hypothalamus can alter bodily urges and drives, including those related to sex. Other parts of the limbic system may also be damaged, causing disturbances of memory and learning, bodily urges, emotions, and internal body regulations.

The limbic system is connected by nerve circuitry to many other parts of the brain. The connections are associated with chemical substances called neurotransmitters. Neurotransmitters can start, increase, decrease, or stop the activity of the nerve structures to which they are connected. After diffuse head injuries, some neurotransmitters can be either deficient or excessive and therefore produce disruptions in regulatory functions of the brain. For example, excesses of certain neurotransmitters can cause abnormally high blood pressure.

Neurotransmitters appear to play an important role in the interactions of the limbic, hypothalamic, and pituitary systems. Some of the disturbances of sexual function occurring after brain injury are related to this area and may be associated with alterations of the neurotransmitters.[50]

## LOCALIZED (FOCAL) INJURIES

Brain injuries are often the result of penetrating wounds or violent blows to the head. Penetrating injuries cause complications such as infections and seizures. As with combined diffuse and localized injuries, the localized injuries may include the various kinds of bleeding, bruises, lacerations, and swelling that we have already described. Localized injury may appear directly beneath the site of a blow (coup injury),[51] or the blow can cause the brain to be displaced against the inner skull on the opposite side, producing a contrecoup injury.[52] Sometimes a coup and a contrecoup injury may occur with the same blow (Fig. 18). Any brain injury resulting in skull fractures or penetration that creates a direct continuity between the scalp and brain tissue is called an *open head injury*.[53] All other brain injuries are *closed*.[54]

## MILD HEAD INJURIES

Mild or minor brain injuries account for the majority of all brain injuries and often do not require hospitalization. Mild head injuries, with brief or absent unconsciousness, usually show no evident signs of injury to the brain on physical examination or other routine studies, including x-rays. These mild traumas, called concussions, were formerly regarded as brief interruptions of brain function without actual brain damage. We now know that brain injury *can*

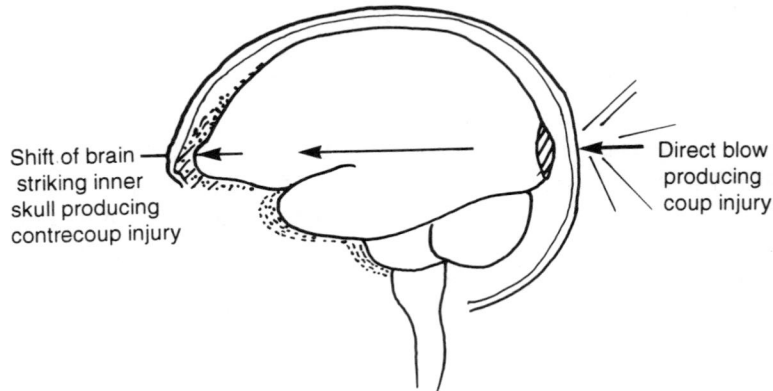

**Figure 18.** Mechanism of coup and contrecoup injuries to the brain.

occur with concussion, although the injury may only be detected by microscopic examination or by special x-ray techniques such as nuclear magnetic resonance imaging (NMRI)[55] of the brain.

# Factors in Recovery

Recovery after severe brain injury is seldom complete. Depending on the nature, severity, location, and extent of injury, permanent physical and mental deficits may be mild to severe. An early measure of the severity of injury is the Glasgow Coma Scale[56] (Table 4). This scale is a summary of the bedside examination and scoring of three activities: eye opening, movement, and speech or sounds. It indicates the level of coma, or level of awareness of the injured person, and allows classification in three levels of severity of injury: mild, moderate, and severe. Other early and repeated bedside examinations help further in determining the nature and degree of injury. The examinations include evaluation of the pupils of the eyes by measuring their size and response to light and their movements in response to turning the head. Examinations also include running cool or warm water in the ear canals, measuring body temperature, blood pressure, pulse, breathing rate and rhythm, and the like. Additional information is obtained by CT scan, magnetic resonance imaging (MRI) of the brain, monitoring of intracranial pressure (ICP), and the length of time after injury that day-to-day memory loss persists (posttraumatic amnesia, PTA).[57] Other factors that influence recovery include the presence of previous brain disease or injury, the promptness and excellence of medical-surgical care, the patient's age, and the presence of other injuries and complications. There are indications that some of these factors influence the type and severity of remaining deficits in sexual function.

**Table 4**

**GLASCOW COMA SCALE (BEST RESPONSE)**

| Eye Opening | | Motor Response | | Verbal Response | |
|---|---|---|---|---|---|
| 4 | Eyes open | 6 | Limb(s) move on command | 5 | Sensible, unconfused speech |
| 3 | Eyes open on request | 5 | Limb(s) move purposefully to avoid pain | 4 | Sensible but confused speech |
| 2 | Eyes open to pain | 4 | Limb(s) bend in almost purposeful way to pain | 3 | Speech makes no sense, but is intelligible |
| 1 | Eyes remain shut in response to all stimuli | 3 | Limb(s) bend reflexly to pain | 2 | Unintelligible voice sounds |
| | | 2 | Limbs straighten reflexly to pain | 1 | No voice sounds |
| | | 1 | No limb movement in response to any stimulus | | |

Highest score = 15 (Does not mean that a patient is normal)

Lowest score (if alive) = 3

Coma: 7 or less is always coma, some 8s are in coma. Definition of coma: no eye opening, no purposeful movement, no intelligible words.

Severe head injury = 3–8 (also if coma lasts 6 or more hours).

Moderate head injury = 9–12

Mild head injury = 13–15

Although these factors allow predictions to be made about the possibilities of survival, they are less precise in predicting the eventual level of survivor recovery. There are many individual variations in the recovery process that make each survivor different from any other. With milder head injuries, recovery may be more rapid, more complete, and even total.

Psychological and social factors play an important role in eventual outcomes. The before-injury mental and personality characteristics of the person, his or her education, training, work experiences, interpersonal and social skills, attitudes and beliefs, and family and community resources all influence recovery. Obviously these factors, as well as before-injury sexual experience, attitudes, and beliefs, will help determine sexual outcomes. A stable, loving relationship that exists before the injury and continues afterward is a great asset.

# Stages of Recovery

Many families have difficulty understanding the process of recovery. During early stages of recovery, the family's greatest concerns focus on whether their loved one will live and if and when he or she will waken from coma. Recovery generally occurs in progressive stages or levels. These stages do not always proceed in a predictable step-by-step pattern. Secondary brain damage due to infection, swelling, delayed bleeding, or seizures, and complications of associated injuries or other medical-surgical problems can greatly alter the recovery pattern. Nevertheless, families can help the medical team in plotting the course of recovery by their observations and understanding of the situation. Many times families may be the first to notice changes in their injured member's condition. Family members can document the recovery process in order to provide information not only for medical personnel, but for the injured person, who likely will have no recollection of the early stages of recovery. Photographs and journals can be helpful to the injured relative as he or she later comes to terms with a vastly changed life-style.

The Rancho Los Amigos Cognitive Scale provides a useful description of eight levels of behavior of the recovering injured person (Table 5). Many rehabilitation programs use the scale to assist both professionals and families in better understanding the recovery process. The scale determines the current level of functioning, what is to be expected, and the implications for types of treatment.

**Table 5**

## STAGES OF RECOVERY: RANCHO LOS AMIGOS COGNITIVE SCALE

---

   I. No response
  II. Generalized response
 III. Localized response
  IV. Confused, agitated
   V. Confused, inappropriate
  VI. Confused, appropriate
 VII. Automatic, appropriate
VIII. Purposeful, appropriate

---

Level I describes a person who does not respond to anything or who appears to be asleep. Many experts believe that we should be careful about what is said around someone who appears to be comatose. In some cases that person may hear, understand, and remember what has been said. A calm, positive atmosphere may be important to the recovery process and certainly can help the family cope better.

At level II the person may react in a general, nonpurposeful way to environmental stimuli such as noise or pain. For example, he or she may groan when pinched or blink when the bedpan is dropped. Movement and behavior do not vary much, but do not routinely occur after the same stimuli. The individual may appear to be sleeping or looking about randomly.

Level III indicates that the person displays purposeful responses, even at times following simple commands or requests such as "open your eyes." The eyes may focus on objects. Speech or gestures can appear. Families can help by responding to needs and encouraging consistent responses of language and activities. Their very presence provides reassurance to the loved one.

Level IV is a difficult stage for everyone. The individual

is growing more alert and active, but increasingly confused and disturbed. The patient may say things that make little sense. Memory is usually limited to the immediate moment. Disorientation to time, place, and person is likely. Aggressive, violent behavior is possible, often without provocation. It is at this level that the following sexually inappropriate behaviors begin to appear: exposure, masturbation, fondling, propositioning, and using foul or abusive language. How upsetting this scene can be for family and friends! In these circumstances the treatment team and family must be mutually supportive in providing a consistent, calm environment for the person. By dealing with the confusion, much of the agitation may subside. Constant repetition of basic information (who? when? what happened?) guides the person to reality and minimizes fear and anxiety.

Later in level IV the individual may perform some basic self-care activities such as eating, brushing teeth, and bathing. Usually the person cannot organize or direct his behavior. The family may be frustrated by such glimpses of the person and hope to again engage in old patterns of relating. For instance, a spouse may expect demonstrations of affection before the injured person is capable of this behavior.

To reduce family exhaustion, simple rotating schedules for visiting and responsibility sharing among family and friends is of value. Staff members often rely upon the family to assist with supervision of the person whose judgment and safety awareness are poor. Counseling and educational-training programs prepare the family for these roles, and assure family members that agitated behaviors are not directed personally toward anyone. Family members and partners may need reminders and support in meeting their own needs such as eating properly, resting, and exercising adequately. They also may need help in obtaining relief from chores such as cooking, driving, picking up mail, and so forth.

At the next stage, level V, agitation decreases. The person is now more able to relate to external events. Although there is a greater level of cooperation, bizarre behaviors and comments persist. The injured person still does not fully understand what has happened, and is unaware of many problems. Concern may be limited to physical problems such as difficulty in walking. Disorientation persists, requiring repeated reminders concerning time, place, and person. Difficulties with memory and thinking become more evident as the person's ability to communicate improves. There may be large gaps in memory of before-injury events (long-term memories). Some individuals believe that they are much younger than their actual age. They may not recognize their spouse, or recall key family events that have occurred during the memory-gap period. Before-injury memory might improve rapidly, slowly, or not at all. Prediction of improvement is difficult or impossible. The process is best monitored by careful observations by the treatment team and family, with close communication between both.

Sexually inappropriate behaviors may decrease during level V. Consistent, clear, and brief statements to the person, by all concerned, will clarify what behaviors are unacceptable. For example, touching the genitalia is not permissible in the presence of company; it is an activity requiring privacy.

If the brain-injured person has difficulty in speaking, gestures or written information can be substituted for the spoken word. It is best to keep questions simple or answerable with a "yes" or "no" response. Family can be educated and trained in the best means of communication. Brief, clear statements are easier for the injured person to understand, and frequent repetition is often necessary in the case of memory deficits.

At level VI bizarre behaviors may become less frequent or disappear. The person becomes more aware of his condition and his own errors. Although serious memory problems may continue, some activities may be remembered. Long-term memory of before-injury events may improve as well. The person is now more capable of relearning old skills. However, attention span may remain very brief.

During level VII, persons become more aware of their

limitations, particularly their physical restrictions. They may be well oriented to their environment. However, they act robotlike in their daily routines. Supervision is still necessary to compensate for decreased judgment and problem-solving ability. Social relationships are still marked by dependency. The injured person may assume a childlike role. For the spouse or partner, the caregiver or parent, this change in roles creates particular stress and can damage the future relationship if not gradually reversed as progress is made. Families will benefit from education and training regarding encouragement of independence at the level of capability of the injured person and discouragement of unnecessary dependence. Family members need to know when to assist and when to ''step back with hands folded.''

Level VIII describes someone who can function independently, essentially without supervision. But less obvious problems such as the lack of full insight into the condition and impaired judgement and abstract reasoning skills often remain. These problems are most apparent to family and friends who spend considerable time with the person. At this stage of recovery plans to reenter community life and return to work more fully evolve. The individual generally has goals and plans for the future. Yet many survivors function at reduced levels in society because of remaining cognitive, emotional, and behavioral changes. These deficits are the basis for long-term rehabilitative and maintenance services for survivors and families.

Not all of the eight stages of recovery may appear in a particular patient. One or more of the stages may be skipped, or the stages may occur in a different sequence than the usual one described. Furthermore, recovery may be arrested at a particular stage or regress to an earlier stage under stresses such as medical or psychological complications.

# Neurological Impairments Relating to Sexuality

Before reviewing the types of problems that may result from brain injury, we should point out that people with head injury have many strengths. These assets can be identified and exploited by the rehabilitation team, the family, and the injured person as they share information. The remaining or enhanced assets, such as physical, psychological, and social skills and resources, can often counterbalance disabilities. Such assets provide a basis for many coping and adaptive skills that enable the brain-injured person to regain a productive, satisfying life.

In focusing on problems that can affect sexuality, we do not want to ignore the injured person's assets. Among the strongest of these is the sustained loving support of the family.

## PROBLEMS ASSOCIATED WITH DOMINANT CEREBRAL HEMISPHERE INJURY

Injuries involving the dominant cerebral hemisphere, usually the left brain, can result in aphasia.[58] This problem in producing speech can range from occasional difficulty in saying desired words, hesitancy or stammering, mispronouncing or saying the wrong words, telegraphing sentences into "bare bones" phrases ("I go store,") to only being able to make a few repetitive automatic words or sounds. Problems in understanding speech can range from trouble with comprehending a series of expressed ideas and difficulty with abstract expressions, to nearly total inability to understand anything that is said. Understanding may be helped by "reading" the speaker's tone of voice, facial expression, and body movement or posture. Often difficulties in writing and reading (dysgraphia,[59] agraphia,[60] and alexia[61]) occur with the speech problems.

Obviously, such difficulties in communicating can profoundly affect the social activities of dating, courting, love-making, and other forms of intimacy. Any of these activities can be effectively thwarted by the frustrations, embarrassment, or shame of the injured person; or the partner may be overwhelmed by the communication barriers. The language of love is as simple as saying "I love you," as complex as the delicate signals that indicate that a person is, or is not, ready for lovemaking, and as intimate as knowing what is, or is not, mutually pleasurable about the act of love.

Injury to the motor and sensory strips and surrounding brain tissues can cause weakness or paralysis of muscles, poor control of posture and movements, and impaired or altered sensation of the opposite sides of the face and body (hemiparesis,[62] hemiplegia,[63] and hemisensory deficit[64]). The disorders of posture and movement may be accompanied by spasticity,[65] and can cause loss of balance, deformed postures, lack of control of limbs or body, pain, problems with keeping the deformed areas clean, and occasionally injury to the person, or to another in close contact.

These sorts of problems can influence sexual functioning directly by interfering with mobility, balance in assuming positions for sexual activities, and the use of one's upper limbs in holding, caressing, manually exploring, undressing, applying contraceptives, and supporting body weight. Muscle spasms can be disruptive to sexual acts, causing minor injury or causing the penis to become dislodged from the vagina. Poor control of oral musculature may produce drooling.

A problem closely related to paralysis is a condition called apraxia.[66] The person with this disorder is unable to perform voluntary activities on request, in spite of understanding the request and wishing to comply with it. And yet the person may be able to spontaneously perform the activity without conscious thought of doing it. Apraxia can have a profound effect on sexual behavior. Actions affected may involve kissing, sucking, hugging, caressing, undressing, applying birth control measures, positioning oneself on the bed, imitating another person's actions, and so forth. The cosmetic effects of these movement and posture disorders may discourage an injured person or partner. Anxiety about the possible occurrence of the disorders may lead to impotence or refusal to attempt lovemaking.

Sensory changes may include decrease or near absence of sensations of touch, pressure, pain, temperature, position of body parts, and vibration. Thus, the affected half of the body may not respond to touch, massage, caressing, hugging, kissing, pinching, or other stimuli applied to the skin. These acts may not produce sexual arousal if they are confined to the affected half of the body. Furthermore, a person with profound loss of sensation is susceptible to skin injury because there is no recognition of pain (as from biting) or prolonged pressure (as from lying in one position for several hours). Limbs that have little sensation are especially clumsy, even if they retain good muscle movements, when the person is unable to substitute vision for the missing sensation (as in a darkened room). Sometimes the affected side of the body is excessively sensitive to touch or sensations may feel peculiar or unpleasant. These affected areas may include the external sexual organs, making sexual acts uncomfortable unless stimulation of the involved side is avoided.

Disturbances of vision may be present, presenting most frequently as hemianopsia[67] in the right field of vision (Fig. 19). With this visual problem, people usually learn to compensate by repeatedly turning their head to the blind side so that they can locate objects on that side in the intact left field of vision. Their movements may be puzzling to others who do not know the reason for them. If the partially blind person is forgetful or distracted from performing the head turns, he may lose track of visual events on the affected side. Dating or sexual activity can be such distractions.

People with dominant hemisphere injuries often feel depressed and anxious at the same time. These feelings may interfere with sexual desire and performance. Depression and anxiety can cause impotence[68] or decreased arousal in women. The same feelings can contribute to lowered self-esteem and self-confidence. Socialization and dating may be impossible hurdles for the teenager with depression and anxiety.

The problems relating to prefrontal lobe and temporal-limbic injuries will be discussed separately because these

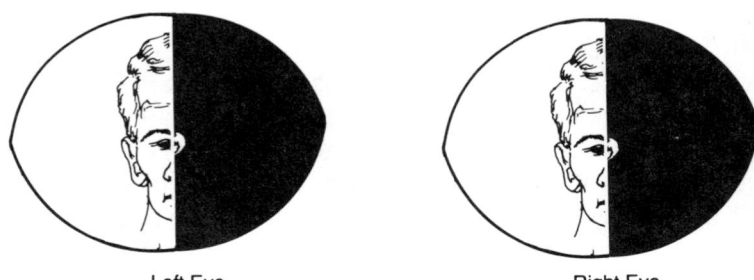

Left Eye                                    Right Eye

**Figure 19.** Hemianopsia is the loss of half of the normal field vision, in this case, the right.

injuries frequently occur as local damage to both sides of those two areas of the brain.

## PROBLEMS ASSOCIATED WITH NONDOMINANT CEREBRAL HEMISPHERE INJURY

The right brain is the nondominant side for most of us, as mentioned previously. Impairments resulting from damage on the nondominant side may include the motor and sensory problems described with dominant brain injury, but they will occur on the *left* side of the body. When visual field losses occur, they generally involve the left half of each eye's field of sight.

Problems with communication, when present, are quite different than those arising from dominant brain injuries. Persons with nondominant brain injury may speak in a monotone, seemingly without emotion (aprosody[69]). Their eye contact is often poor. They may be unaware of the rules of polite conversation, tending to stand too close, interrupt the other speaker, and not allow others "equal time." They may talk excessively, fail to come to the point, switch abruptly to other topics, and be disorganized in presenting their ideas. People with right brain injuries often fail to appreciate the subtleties of what others say. Frequently they are concrete in their interpretations. "The grass is always greener on the other side of the street" may mean just that to them. They may miss the meaning of facial expression, body movements and gestures, and the little variations of tone of voice or inflection that change the meaning of what is said, or are substituted for speech. They may be unable to express or understand humor.

Reading and writing are subject to disturbances such as difficulty in scanning, poor handwriting, skipping lines, failure to visually track to the left margin of the page, and letter reversals and confusions.

In summary, the problems of language and communication are often more subtle in nondominant hemisphere injuries than in dominant hemisphere injuries. Nevertheless, the problems can prove to be formidable and frustrating to the person with brain injury, the family, and partner. The language of socialization, courtship, and love is often unspoken, hinted at, and embellished by gestures, facial expressions, and body language that may neither be expressed nor received by the individual with these deficits. Language may be misinterpreted. For example, "I feel like retiring," said with a come-hither smile might be answered, "Well, goodnight," thus missing the gentle cue for lovemaking.

Persons with nondominant brain injuries are prone to any of a number of disturbances in perception.[70] They can neglect the entire left side of the external environment despite having normal hearing, vision, or other sensations on that side. In addition, the left side of the body may be ignored. Parts of the body may not be recognized (autotopagnosia[71]), or may be thought to be someone else's. Some people with injuries of the nondominant brain are unaware of their injury or of the resulting impairments (anosagnosia[72]). For example, they do not recognize that their left side is paralyzed. Others have trouble judging distances, sizes of objects, speed of moving objects, and when something (including their own body) is aligned properly, for instance straight up and down instead of on a tilt. As a result of such visual distortions, people may be clumsy or inaccurate of movement, hang onto walls, lose balance and fall. They can become lost in familiar places, even their own homes. Occasionally they are unable to recognize familiar faces and undressing may be utterly confusing. They may be unable to tell left from right. Even if sensations of touch, pressure, movement, temperature, and pain are intact, the person may not be able to detect the shape, consistency, size, or other identifying characteristics so as to be able to name an object in their hand (astereognosis).[73] Sometimes sensations are distorted. For example, a hand may feel swollen, heavy, or "dead." Some people lose the ability to sing, play music, or appreciate it. Shakespeare called music "the food of love." For many people, music and dancing are a vital part of courtship, and may be a strong stimulus for arousal. Imagine the effect of losing touch with half of your world and half of your body! Imagine not being able to recognize parts of your partner's body or parts of your own! Unless you learn to become aware of and compensate for these deficits, or have a partner who learns techniques such as approaching you from the other side, frustration and confusion can occur during preparatory activities or sexual acts. Arousal may be thwarted by inadequate or unpleasant stimuli. Seemingly bizarre interpretations of sensory events can effectively inhibit a budding relationship long before intimacy beings.

People with nondominant brain injuries often are "flat," that is, they appear to be without strong or varied emotions. Sometimes, although the external appearance, facial expression and body language sends this message, people do not actually feel indifferent. Instead, they can feel sorrowful or moody and swiftly change from sadness to gaiety or silliness. They tend to be less cautious and anxious about their condition than people with dominant brain injuries. In fact they are often impulsive and indifferent to precarious situations because of the neglect or denial of their disabilities. Thus they may "wade" into sexual behaviors and activities without precautions. On the other hand, they may be indifferent to the point of having no interest in close relationships; they may be so distractible that they cannot attend to or concentrate on what a partner is trying to communicate.

With injuries to either cerebral hemisphere, major difficulties may arise in cognitive[74] functions such as awareness of, and orientation to, environment, memory, learning, problem solving, speed of processing information, and other intellectual processes. These difficulties occur in addition to the perceptual and language disorders we have already described. Obviously such problems can affect sexuality in many ways. They are often the basis for frustration, despondency, and other psychological reactions that destroy self-esteem and alienate intimate partners and friends. They complicate efforts to educate and train people in regaining social and sexual skills. Consider some of the consequences of severe recent memory deficits such as forgetting the contraceptive or insisting on repetitive sexual activity because of inability to remember the activity must be completed. These mental problems and the resulting psychological and social consequences have usually created the greatest difficulties in attaining satisfactory sexual function after brain injury.

## PROBLEMS ASSOCIATED WITH PREFRONTAL AREA INJURIES

Damage to the prefrontal cortex (Fig. 20), the areas of frontal lobes in front of the motor-controlling segments, occurs frequently, often on both sides. When injury is confined to the undersurface, that person is likely to be impulsive, exhibit disinhibitions,[75] and lack control of what he or she says and does. Attention and concentration are limited, with ready diversion by other events. The individual is restless and easily provoked, sometimes to abusive and even violent behavior. Judgment and safety awareness may be impaired. Usually the person is not readily aroused sexually, and males may have difficulties with erection and release of semen. Less often, heightened sexual interest, coupled with explosive moods, may lead to aggressive or violent sexual behavior.

Injuries of the outer and upper surface of the prefrontal area (Fig. 20) are likely to produce a disinterested, dull-appearing, sleepy individual who is unable to make decisions, thinks and performs slowly, and has difficulty initiating ideas or activity (abulia[76]). Occasionally, such a person

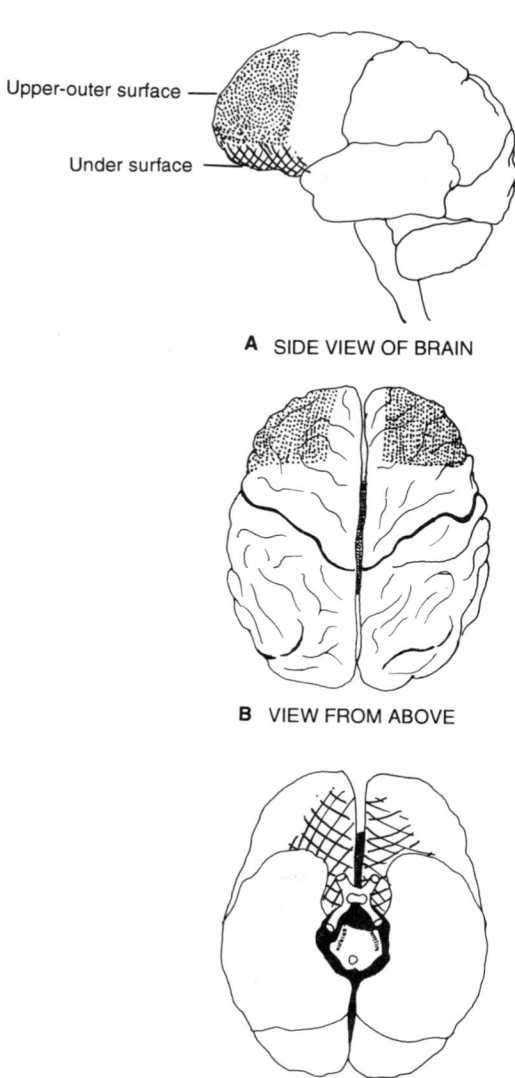

Upper-outer surface

Under surface

**A** SIDE VIEW OF BRAIN

**B** VIEW FROM ABOVE

**C** VIEW FROM BELOW

**Figure 20.** The prefrontal areas of the brain (*shaded*), viewed from (A) left, (B) above, and (C) below.

will seem "frozen" into inactivity and silence. As a result, there may be little or no interest in sexual matters, and yet sexual responses such as erection and vaginal lubrication are usually preserved.

More extensive injuries of the prefrontal area can cause the person to have features of both undersurface and upper-outer surface injuries. The person can be childish, silly, inappropriate in social behavior, and selfish. Other problems may include inability to plan ahead; limited display of fantasy, thought, and speech; difficulty in sequencing thoughts of activities; and slovenliness. The person may act as if there is no conscience, and display flat, shallow emotions, seeming depression, and endless repetition of speech or actions (perseveration[77]).

People with these prefrontal injuries may be inappropriately sexually uninhibited. Some may expose themselves and publicly masturbate. Others may solicit sexual activity from anyone in their company, resorting to vulgar language and fondling, with indifference or even amusement at the distress of those they abuse. More often, however, there is more "talk" than explicit abuse. In fact either sex may have difficulty becoming sexually aroused and impotence may occur.

Despite these changes in behavior, thought, and emotion, many people with prefrontal injuries may perform well on standardized intelligence tests. They are often described by family or friends as "changed people." It is the personality itself that has changed.

## PROBLEMS ASSOCIATED WITH TEMPORAL LOBE AND LIMBIC INJURIES

Injuries to this region of the brain (Figs. 12 and 13) can cause disturbances of taste, smell, and hearing. When both temporal lobes are involved the injuries can affect memory, learning, behavior, emotion, basic drives, and the endocrine glands.[78] Thus sexuality can be compromised in various ways. The dominant, usually right, temporal lobe increases its electrical activity dramatically in healthy people during intense sexual activity and orgasms. Seizures on that side may be associated with sensations of sexual excitement and orgasm. Injury to an area of the limbic system known as the septum[79] can cause impotence.

Temporal lobe seizures account for about 20 percent of all types of late (occurring later than one week after injury) seizures.

Temporal lobe seizures present in various forms, which are summarized in Table 6. Occasionally nonspecific sexually oriented behavior may accompany seizure activities. For instance, the person may utter repetitive, meaningless vul-

**Table 6**

## FREQUENT SIGNS AND SYMPTOMS OF LIMBIC-TEMPORAL LOBE SEIZURES

- Unusual sensations
    Strange or unpleasant tastes or odors
    Seeing objects as smaller or larger than their actual size
- Internal disorders
    Abdominal cramps and gurgling
    Irregular heart beat
    Nausea and sweating
- Strange feelings
    "I've been here before" (in a new place)
    "I've never been here before" (in a familiar place)
    States of rage, dreaminess, dissociation, fear, elation, and
        sorrow
- Strange behavior
    Repetitive, automatic walking, running, and lip smacking
    Acting crazy

garities or engage in isolated pelvic thrusts. In all of these variations, postseizure confusion and drowsiness with no memory of preceding events is the rule. Excessive sexual behavior is not present between seizures. In fact, most people with temporal lobe seizures have decreased sexual interest and activity between fits. But some people with temporal lobe injuries display unusual between-seizure behaviors such as exhibitionism,[80] changes in male or female preference, transvestism,[81] or fetishism.[82]

Often people with temporal lobe seizures have hormonal disorders related to pituitary gland misfunctions. Men may experience reduced sex drive. They may lose function of the testicles, becoming impotent, sterile, and deficient in secondary sex characteristics such as facial hair. They may also exhibit enhanced breast development. Women can have reduced ovarian function, causing menses to stop (amenorrhea[83]) or become irregular. They may become infertile, experience decreased vaginal lubrication, and lose secondary female characteristics such as breast development. Some women develop polycystic ovaries,[84] or produce breast milk.

Injuries to the front part of both temporal lobes may result in the Kluver-Bucy syndrome.[85] Persons with this syndrome eat excessively, place all kinds of objects into their mouths, are extremely docile, ignore or deny visual stimuli without evidence of loss of vision, and display overly sexual behavior (often repetitively masturbating). The syndrome is not as rare as previously thought. It is often partial, may disappear over time, and responds favorably to the antiseizure drug carbamazapine (Tegretol).

## PROBLEMS ASSOCIATED WITH OCCIPITAL LOBE INJURIES

Injuries to the occipital lobes (Fig. 14), the area of the back of the brain, occur less frequently than frontal or temporal lobe injuries. Occipital lobe injuries may result in visual deficits varying from visual field cut[86] (for example, loss of half sight in each eye) to cortical blindness[87] when both sides are damaged. Cortical blindness is often less than total, with some ability to detect rapid movements in the periphery of the visual fields. There is no damage to the eyes or to the nerves of the eyes. The condition frequently improves as spontaneous recovery proceeds. On occasion, the blindness is accompanied by denial of deficient vision and making up of stories about what is "seen." Such denial, or associated deficits resulting from brain injury to other areas, may hamper a specific visual rehabilitation program.

Visual impairments may not directly interfere with sexual activities if the impaired person has attained good compensatory skills of other intact sensory systems, especially touch and hearing. However, psychological reactions of the person or others can pose problems of self-image, self-esteem, and interpersonal relationships that affect sexuality.

## PROBLEMS ASSOCIATED WITH BASAL GANGLIA INJURIES

Injuries to the basal ganglia (Fig. 15) produce disorders of willed movement. Parkinsonian syndrome,[88] the most frequently occurring pattern of deficits, consists of rigidity,[89] tremor, and slow movement. Other movement disorders stemming from injuries to parts of the basal ganglia are spontaneous flinging of the arms or legs (ballism[90]), or prolonged bizarre movement disorders such as athetosis,[91] chorea,[92] and dystonia.[93] These movement disorders usually are transient, but in rare cases may persist. They can interfere with willed movements or postures, disturb balance, create progressive limb deformities, and be associated with facial grimacing, indistinct speech, or drooling. Thus, such movement disorders can disturb sexual activity, create cosmetic problems, and be psychologically tormenting for either partner.

Emotional tension often aggravates the movement disorders.

## PROBLEMS ASSOCIATED WITH THALAMIC INJURIES

Injuries to the thalamus (Fig. 16) result in loss of sense of touch, pressure, position, pain, and temperature. The effects of such loss on sexual function have already been described. One thalamic disorder, termed the thalamic pain[94] syndrome, produces a recurring sensation of pain over one half of the body and is accompanied by extreme emotional distress. In many cases thalamic pain is triggered by touching the affected side. People with this syndrome are often so depressed that they lose interest in sex.

## PROBLEMS ASSOCIATED WITH HYPOTHALAMIC AND PITUITARY INJURIES

Hypothalamus and/or pituitary gland injury (Fig. 16) is frequently associated with severe brain trauma. In children, delay or absence of puberty, or precocious puberty,[95] may occur. Adults may have reduced ovarian or testicular function that produces sex hormone deficiencies and infertility. We spoke of these problems in the earlier discussion of hormonal changes with temporal lobe injuries.

Pituitary gland failure can cause excessive loss of body fluids via the kidneys despite enormous increases in the amount of fluids swallowed (diabetes insipidus[96]). Target organs of the pituitary other than the primary sex glands may also be inadequately stimulated and therefore fail (for example, the adrenal or thyroid glands). The pituitary may produce a hormone called prolactin[97] in excessive amounts, causing enlargement of breast tissue, production of breast milk, impotence, and failure to ovulate.

In addition to these hormonal disorders, injuries in the

vicinity of the hypothalamus can cause disturbances in body temperature, heart rate, blood pressure, and breathing. The injured person may have episodes of fever, irregular or rapid heart and breathing rate, or high blood pressure. These episodes can occur in isolation or in combinations. The natural increases in blood pressure, pulse, and respiration that occur during sexual excitement may become exaggerated in people with injuries in the vicinity of the hypothalamus. Excessive appetite and progressive obesity may occur with hypothalamic disturbance. Decreased libido[98] is also possible.

We have previously mentioned the role of neurotransmitters in the brain, and that brain injury sometimes causes alteration of these chemicals. Alterations of certain of these chemicals can produce deficiencies of hypothalamic or pituitary function, just as if those two sites were directly injured. The hormonal problems we described with temporal lobe seizures may also be caused by these chemical changes.

## PROBLEMS ASSOCIATED WITH CEREBELLAR INJURIES

Injuries to the cerebellum (Fig. 5) cause clumsy, fragmented, uncoordinated willed movements (ataxia[99]), spontaneous jerking of the eyes (nystagmus[100]), tremor of the limbs, dysarthria,[101] and loss of balance.

People with cerebellar disorders are sometimes mistakenly considered to be drunk. The difficulties in motor control create psychological problems and mechanical difficulties with sexual activities that are similar to those of people with the previously discussed movement disorders.

## PROBLEMS ASSOCIATED WITH BRAINSTEM INJURIES

Injuries to the brainstem (Fig. 16) can affect any of the systems housed in its three parts: midbrain, pons, and medulla.

Damage to the reticular activating system may produce prolonged coma. Less severe damage to that system can disturb wake-sleep cycles, cause extreme sleepiness and difficulty in rousing from sleep, and inattentiveness and inability to concentrate.

Brainstem injuries may result in damage to one or several of the cranial nerves (3 through 12) that originate in the brainstem (Table 3). Damage is particularly common to nerves 3, 4, and 6, which govern eye movements. The usual result is weakness or paralysis of one or more of the muscles providing eye movement. The effects include double vision, cosmetic defects due to unsynchronized eye movements, or drooping eyelid. Facial nerve injuries also create cosmetic problems due to weakness or paralysis of muscles that are used in facial expression. Inability to close the eyelid and to produce tears may lead to infection and damage to the eye. Early treatment of double vision or incomplete eyelid closure in the form of eye patching may be cosmetically distressing to the wearer. Drooling is another unpleasant effect of facial nerve injury.

Acoustic nerve injury can result in deafness on the affected side, or dizziness. This dizziness is actually a sensation of spinning, or having the immediate environment spinning around you (vertigo[102]), and is often associated with faintness and nausea. The spinning is aggravated by vigorous movements or certain positions of the head, such as can occur in sexual activities.

Injuries to the glossopharyngeal nerve may cause difficulty with swallowing and taste. Vagus nerve injuries also can interfere with swallowing (dysphagia[103]), as well as with clarity of speech, and voice production. Injury to the accessory nerve causes weakness of neck and shoulder blade muscles, sometimes producing a weak, unstable, drooping, and painful shoulder, Damage to the hypoglossal nerve can weaken or paralyze tongue muscles, thus interfering with intelligibility of speech, eating, and swallowing. In summary, cranial nerve injuries can directly affect sexuality, with dizziness, or shoulder weakness; but can also have an indirect effect by creating communications or cosmetic problems that can be dispiriting unless treatment is made available.

Damage to the pons (Fig. 5) can cause a person to become paralyzed in all four limbs (quadriplegia[104]) and lose function of many of the cranial nerves. The individual with this injury is unable to speak or swallow, but is usually able to move the eyes and, if there is no major damage to the brain proper, will be alert and otherwise mentally intact. This group of signs is called the "locked-in" syndrome.[105] In its pure form, as just described, it is quite rare after head injury, but more often is seen as a partial syndrome along with other brain damage. The person with "locked-in" syndrome may be so incapacitated that sexual activity can only be experienced as a passive, dependent partner.

## PROBLEMS ASSOCIATED WITH MILD BRAIN INJURIES

Our discussion of brain injuries thus far has been primarily concerned with more severe injuries, both diffuse and focal.[106] Now we will consider the effects of mild or "minor" brain injury, which may be defined as an early Glasgow Coma Score of 13 or better. A score of 13 indicates that the patient is conscious, has willed movement, can open the eyes, and speaks understandably. Often recovery following mild head injury is rapid, over hours or days, and complete. However, many people with mild head injury may continue to complain of symptoms that are characteristic of the postconcussion syndrome.[107] The syndrome may be short-lived, or it may persist for many months. Complaints include lightheadedness or dizziness, headaches (which are often aggravated by sexual activity), and a number of other symptoms which are listed in Table 7.

Previous impressions that these patients were psycho-

**Table 7**

## TYPES OF COMPLAINTS WITH POSTCONCUSSION SYNDROME

Light-headedness
Dizziness, vertigo
Headaches
Double vision
Blurred vision
Ringing in ears
Hard of hearing
Memory problems
Trouble concentrating
Distractable
Tired out
Anxious
Excessive sweating
Sad
Trouble sleeping
Moody
Irritable
Changes in menstrual periods
Impaired vaginal lubrication
Impotence
Not interested in sex

logically unstable have been modified in light of evidence that there are microscopic changes in the injured brain, and that neuropsychological tests may indicate signs of organic mental dysfunctions. The incidence of decreased sex drive or impotence is reported in nearly 50 percent of cases. We do not know whether most of the cases of impotence are men-
(*text continued on p. 71*)

**Table 8**

## POSSIBLE EFFECTS OF BRAIN INJURY ON SEXUALITY

### Problems Associated with Dominant Hemisphere Injuries
### (Usually left side of brain)

| Functions | Impairments | Effect on Sexuality |
|---|---|---|
| *Language and communication* | Problems in producing speech:<br>Finding the right words<br>Difficulty saying the correct words<br>Hesitancy, stammering, or mispronouncing<br>Reduced phrases or repetitive phrases<br>Problems in understanding speech:<br>Comprehending expressed ideas<br>Understanding abstract language (more complicated language) | May be unable to express affection in writing or in words<br>Diminished social abilities<br>Miscommunication and misunderstandings<br>Frustration and embarrassment<br>May be perceived as childlike and treated like a child, altering the feelings between partners<br>Diminished ability to arouse partner by love words, stimulating phrases, and verbal demonstrations of affection |

(*continued*)

**Table 8**

**POSSIBLE EFFECTS OF BRAIN INJURY ON SEXUALITY** (*Continued*)

| Functions | Impairments | Effect on Sexuality |
|---|---|---|
| | Understanding written language: poor handwriting, skipping lines, poor scanning, misreading left side of page | |
| Sensation | Problems with the loss or alteration of feeling of body parts:<br>Susceptible to injury<br>Clumsy<br>May be either overly sensitive or lack feeling<br>Pain | Decreased feeling, affecting ability to be stimulated to arousal<br>Overly sensitive, not wishing to be touched, partner experiences diminished ability to be stimulated<br>Decreased ability to move about without disturbing sexual play |
| Movement | Problems with the loss of ability to command movement (apraxia): | Drooling, lack of ability to kiss and caress with mouth<br>Lack of control of limbs, spasms disrupt |

| | | |
|---|---|---|
| | Muscle spasms | sex acts, and can cause accidental injury |
| | Weakness and fatigability of muscles | Problems with bed mobility limiting balance in assuming positions during sex acts |
| | Poor control of movements and uncoordination | Pain |
| | Poor control of posture | Problems with holding, caressing, and undressing |
| | | Problem with applying contraception |
| Vision | Loss of right field of vision | Poor vision may result in clumsiness |
| *Emotions/behavior* | Depression | Diminished sexual drive, impotence, or decreased arousal |
| | Anxiety | Poor self-esteem and decreased self-confidence, may not initiate dating, new relationships, or approach partner for sexual pleasure |
| | Changes in hormones, body temperature | Cosmetic problems, may not be as attractive to partner or may have poor self-esteem |
| | | Impulsive behavior due to anxiety interfering with current relationships or prevent attracting new relationships |

*(continued)*

**Table 8**

**POSSIBLE EFFECTS OF BRAIN INJURY ON SEXUALITY** (*Continued*)

| Functions | Impairments | Effect on Sexuality |
|---|---|---|
| | | Changes in body temperature or other basic regulatory functions may result in behaviors perceived as bizarre or unusual by partner |
| *Cognitive* | Poor decision making<br>Poor ability to plan ahead<br>Poor memory, usually short-term and recent events, but sometimes no long-term memories<br>Slowed processing of information | Poor decisions, judgments which can alienate friends and family resulting in decreased opportunities for social relationships or break up of current relationships<br>Poor planning, may interfere with courting and dating behaviors or maintaining relationship<br>Distractibility<br>Memory, may forget just had sex, frustrating partner, or disorganization that limits setting up romantic evenings |

Long-term memory, may not have
special memories that have bonded
relationship over time. May not
remember family members and friends

May forget to use contraception

## Problems Associated with Nondominant Hemisphere Injuries
### (Usually right side of brain; left side of body)

| Functions | Impairments | Effect on Sexuality |
|---|---|---|
| Motor | Same as dominant hemisphere | Same as dominant hemisphere |
| Sensory | Same as dominant hemisphere | Same as dominant hemisphere |
| Visual | Loss of vision in left half of eyes | Same as dominant hemisphere |
| Language | Poor eye contact | Lack of ability to express emotions by changes in voice. May be perceived as not caring, and indifferent to others |
| | Poor communication skills, interrupt others | Poor communication skills result in frustration and anger for partner, family, and friends |
| | Poor at taking turns | |
| | Talk excessively and change topics inappropriately | Misinterpretation and miscommunication cause friction in relationships |
| | Appear disorganized in conversation | |
| | Failure to come to point | |
| | Miss subtleties of conversation | |

*(continued)*

**Table 8**

**POSSIBLE EFFECTS OF BRAIN INJURY ON SEXUALITY** (*Continued*)

| *Functions* | *Impairments* | *Effect on Sexuality* |
| --- | --- | --- |
| | Misread gestures and other cues | |
| | Unable to read and respond to humor | |
| *Perception* | Loss of ability to recognize familiar faces | Loss of sense of balance and depth perception results in clumsy behavior, may alienate partner or cause injury |
| | Loss of ability to distinguish left and right | Loss of a common bond in enjoying music or dancing together |
| | Loss of sense of balance and depth perception | Partner must extensively accommodate unique needs of injured person, and may feel depleted and stressed |
| | Neglect left side of body and environment despite normal hearing and sensation | Arousal decreased by poor stimulation affected by misinterpretation |
| | Inability to detect shape and size of objects held or touched | Partner may need to take role of undressing both themselves and partner |
| | Diminished or lost ability to sing, dance, and enjoy music | |

| Functions | Impairments | Effect on Sexuality |
|---|---|---|
| *Cognitive* | Same as dominant hemisphere | Same as dominant hemisphere |
| *Emotions/Behavior* | Unaware of problems<br>Performs slowly<br>Problem initiating ideas or activities<br>Decreased interest in sex<br>Unable to make decisions<br>Swift changes in mood<br>Impulsive behaviors<br>Distractible | Partner may become frustrated by lack of interest or having to initiate sexual contact or affectionate behaviors<br>Behaviors that let others know that they are cared for may be lacking<br>Stress level for partner may affect their interest in sexual contact<br>Role changes can drain partner and family<br>Lack of initiation can interfere with forming new relationships |

## Problems Associated with Prefrontal Injuries

| Functions | Impairments | Effect on Sexuality |
|---|---|---|
| *Emotions/Behavior* | Impulsive<br>Uninhibited<br>Attention and concentration limited<br>Moody or changeable<br>Poor judgment | Difficulty in relating to others<br>May not be easily aroused<br>Aggressive sexual behavior<br>May perform sexual behavior in wrong place or at wrong time<br>Inappropriate sexual talk |

*(continued)*

**Table 8**

## POSSIBLE EFFECTS OF BRAIN INJURY ON SEXUALITY (*Continued*)

| Functions | Impairments | Effect on Sexuality |
|---|---|---|
| | Impaired safety awareness | May be perceived as a "different person" |
| | | Susceptibility to transmissible infections and pregnancy |

### Problems Associated with Temporal Lobe and Limbic Injuries

| Function | Impairments | Effect on Sexuality |
|---|---|---|
| *Sensation* | Taste and smell | Impaired taste and smell may affect pleasure experienced |
| | Hearing | Hearing problems may result in partner's need to use more gestures |
| *Cognitive* | Memory | |
| | Learning, same as dominant hemisphere | |
| *Emotions/ Behavior* | Seizure activity | Behaviors that accompany seizure may be bizarre |
| | Impotency | |

| Function | Impairments | Effect on Sexuality |
|---|---|---|
| | Eat excessively | Frighten sexual partner making them reluctant to engage in sex |
| | Put objects in mouth | Unable to perform sexually |
| | Behave passively | Sterility |
| | Overly sexual behavior | |
| | Changes in sex hormones | |

## Problems Associated with Occipital Lobe Injuries

| Function | Impairments | Effect on Sexuality |
|---|---|---|
| Visual | Field cuts | May alienate partner |
| | Cortical blindness | Affect self-image and self-esteem |
| | | Clumsy foreplay and sexual activities |

## Problems Associated with Basal Ganglia Injuries

| Function | Impairments | Effect on Sexuality |
|---|---|---|
| Movement | Unable to control movement | May injure partner with uncontrolled movement |
| | | Difficult to get into and maintain sexual positions |
| | | Cosmetic problems may affect attractiveness to others |

(continued)

**Table 8**

## POSSIBLE EFFECTS OF BRAIN INJURY ON SEXUALITY (*Continued*)

### Problems Associated with Thalamic Injuries

| Function | Impairments | Effect on Sexuality |
|----------|-------------|---------------------|
| *Sensation* | Loss of sense of touch, pressure, position, pain, and temperature | Depression<br>Pain associated with touch<br>Decreased arousal |

### Problems Associated with Hypothalamic and Pituitary Gland Injuries

| Function | Impairments | Effect on Sexuality |
|----------|-------------|---------------------|
| *Physical* | In children, absence of puberty or early puberty | Changes in body, enlarged breasts in men |
| | Changes in sex hormones | Impotence |
| | Loss of fluids | Sterility |
| | Changes in basic body regulation such as temperature, blood pressure, and breathing | Lowered self-esteem, less attraction to partner |
| | Obesity | Decreased sex drive |

## Problems Associated with Cerebellar Injuries

| Function | Impairments | Effect on Sexuality |
|---|---|---|
| Movement | Clumsy, uncoordinated movements | Difficulty performing sexual acts |
| | Jerking of eyes | Lowered self-esteem and confidence |
| | Tremor of limbs | May appear drunk to others |
| | Slowed, slurred speech | Inhibit new relationships |
| | Loss of balance | Decreased attractiveness to partner |
| | | Inability to use contraceptives |

## Problems Associated with Brainstem Injuries

| Function | Impairments | Effect on Sexuality |
|---|---|---|
| Physical | Sleep disturbance, lethargy | Appears unattractive and helpless to self or others |
| | Eye movement | Partner must initiate and perform all sexual activity |
| | Facial expression | |
| | Locked-in syndrome | |

## Problems Associated with Mild Head Injury

| Function | Impairments | Effect on Sexuality |
|---|---|---|
| Cognitive | Memory | Disorganization |
| | Trouble concentrating | Distraction from sexual arousal |

*(continued)*

**Table 8**

## POSSIBLE EFFECTS OF BRAIN INJURY ON SEXUALITY (*Continued*)

| Functions | Impairments | Effect on Sexuality |
|---|---|---|
| Vision | Distractible | |
| | Double vision | Distraction from sexual arousal |
| | Blurred vision | |
| Perception | Ringing in ears | Distraction from sexual arousal |
| | Hard of hearing | |
| Emotions/ | Irritable, moody | Impaired relationships |
| Behavior | Tired out | |
| | Anxious, depressed | |
| Physical | Headaches | Decreased interest in sex |
| | Dizziness | Inability to perform |
| | Vertigo | Lowered self-confidence |
| | Excessive sweating | Lowered self-esteem |
| | Sleep disturbances | |
| | Changes in menstrual cycle | |
| | Decreased vaginal lubrication | |
| | Impotence | |

tally or physicaly caused, or are caused by a combination of both mental and physical dysfunction.

It has been said that the brain is the ultimate sexual organ: the seat of sexual urges, thoughts, sensations, inhibitions, and behaviors. By understanding some of the many possible malfunctions of the brain, we can better appreciate the direct and indirect effects these disorders exert on sexuality and sexual function. Table 8 outlines how each of the neurological syndromes we have described affects sexuality.

# Types of Sexual Dysfunction

## CLASSIFICATION

It is helpful to classify sexual disorders according to their cause. This system of classification provides indications of the forms of treatment that are likely to be beneficial for each disorder. Disorders resulting from physical factors are called primary or organic[108] dysfunctions. Primary sexual dysfunctions stemming from brain injury are the result of neurological or hormonal disturbances. Primary dysfunctions are also caused by other physical factors, such as injuries to other parts of the body, medical and surgical complications after injury, and medical problems preceding the injury.

Secondary or functional[109] sexual dysfunctions are caused by psychological or social factors. In brain-injured survivors, these disabilities may result from nonorganic psychological factors arising after the injury such as depression as a reaction to realizing the extent or severity of the lingering effects of the injury.

Pre-existing primary or secondary sexual dysfunctions may persist or may recur following brain injury. If there is a sexual partner, that person may have primary or secondary dysfunctions that contribute to the disabled person's sexual dysfunctions. The responses of family, friends, and society to the disabled person may be the source of secondary dysfunctions long after the original brain injury. Table 9 is a

**Table 9**

## SEXUAL DISABILITIES CLASSIFIED ACCORDING TO THEIR CAUSES

| A. Primary Disabilities (Physical or Organic Causes) | B. Secondary Disabilities (Psychological or Social Causes) |
|---|---|
| 1. Disorders of the brain and/or brainstem; neural and hormonal disturbances (including mental dysfunctions) <br><br> 2. Disorders of part of the rest of the nervous system: <br>   a. Spinal cord disorders <br>   b. Nerve root,[110] nerve plexus,[111] and peripheral nerve[112] disorders <br><br> 3. Injuries to blood vessels that provide circulation to the genital organs <br><br> 4. Other injuries: <br>   a. Musculoskeletal (fractures, crush injuries, and so forth) <br>   b. Head and facial <br><br> 5. Surgical and medical complications <br>   a. Severe malnutrition <br>   b. Prolonged bed rest <br>   c. Drug toxicities and side effects <br>   d. Pain <br>   e. Delayed complications (hydrocephalus,[113] late seizures, and so forth) | 1. Nonorganic problems existing before the brain injury <br>   a. Mental disorders <br>   b. Behavioral disorders <br>   c. Emotional disorders <br>   d. Functional sexual disorders (impotence, dispareunia,[114] and premature ejaculation[115]) <br><br> 2. Nonorganic problems arising from reactions to the brain injury (postinjury reactions) <br>   a. Responses to the consequences of disability <br>   b. Responses to the reactions of others |

detailed list of the types of disabilities, according to their causes.

Another way of classifying sexual disabilities is according to the functional system that is disturbed. Table 10 combines this functional approach with the causative system (shown in Table 9). We emphasize that in many cases, a sexual dysfunction may have more than one physical or psychosocial cause. In Table 10, we have inserted letters after each listed disability, indicating the origin of that disability. The letter "P" denotes primary, "S" secondary, and "B" both primary and secondary.

Using this combined system of classification, we will look at these dysfunctions more closely.

## DISORDERS OF SEX DRIVE AND INTEREST

Disturbance of libido is a frequent finding after head injury; most persons with such a disturbance will have decreased or even absent sex drive and interest. We have previously noted that the decrease may be directly related to changes in brain function. There is growing evidence that hormonal abnormalities and brain chemical neurotransmitter deficiencies or imbalances play a significant role. Any influence that compromises alertness can reduce libido. Brain injury itself can produce sleepiness, as in brainstem damage to the reticular activating system (which normally produces neurotransmitters that stimulate or enhance alertness and wake-sleep cycles) or in upper-outer surface frontal lobe injuries. Many drugs, legal and illicit, can reduce libido, either due to sedation or other effects. Extreme fatigue can produce a similar result. Chronic illness or pain, malnutrition, depression, and anxiety are other causes that may reduce sex drive in some brain-injured persons. Some people with mild brain injury have headaches that may be triggered or aggravated by sexual activity.

We have pointed out that injuries to prefrontal temporal lobes and related limbic structures can produce the less

**Table 10**
## SEXUAL DISABILITIES CLASSIFIED ACCORDING TO THE DISTURBED FUNCTIONAL SYSTEM

| *Functional System* | *Disorder* | *Origin** |
|---|---|---|
| Sex drive/interest | Decreased libido | B |
| | Increased libido | B |
| Sexual response | Impotence or inadequate penile erection | B |
| | Decreased vaginal lubrication and engorgement of clitoris | B |
| | Inability to ejaculate or retrograde ejaculation | P |
| | Premature ejaculation | S |
| | Inability to attain or difficulty in attaining orgasm | B |
| | Painful intercourse (dyspareunia) | B |
| | Vaginismus[116] | B |
| Fertility | Male: Defective or inadequate number of sperm | P |
| | Female: Absence of ovulation, tubal obstruction, vaginal environment hostile to sperm | P |
| Mobility | Difficulty with, or inability to perform transfers, bed mobility, positioning, movement during sexual activity | P |
| Self-care skills | Difficulty with or inability to perform: | |
| | Undressing | P |
| | Hygiene and grooming | B |

*(continued)*

**Table 10**

## SEXUAL DISABILITIES CLASSIFIED ACCORDING TO THE DISTURBED FUNCTIONAL SYSTEM (*Continued*)

| Functional System | Disorder | Origin* |
|---|---|---|
| | Bowel and bladder care | P |
| | Contraceptive use | B |
| Sensation | Diminished or absent sensations in primary or secondary sex organs, hands, and so forth | P |
| | Uncomfortable sensations or pain | P |
| Communication and oral function | Aphasias | P |
| | Dysarthrias and other articulation problems | P |
| | Aphonia[117] | P |
| | Poverty of speech and/or language | P |
| | Poor mouth, tongue, and/or lip control, drooling | P |
| Cosmetic | Facial and/or head defects | P |
| | Other body deformities | P |
| | Movement disorders | P |
| | Bladder-bowel incontinence | P |
| Mental | Intellectual, cognitive and perceptive disorders | P |
| | Behavioral disorders | B |
| | Emotional disorders | B |
| | Personality disorders | B |
| Social | Poor self-image and self-esteem | B |
| | Poor interpersonal skills | B |
| | Poor community skills | B |
| | Poor dating and courting skills | B |

*P = Primary; S = Secondary; B = Both primary and secondary.

commonly occurring state of increased libido. Drugs like alcohol, marijuana, cocaine, and amphetamines may temporarily increase libido. Erotic touch, fantasy, visual, auditory, and other sensory stimuli, particularly when provided by a desirable partner, are effective means of arousal of interest and may counteract some of the factors causing reduced libido.

## DISORDERS OF SEXUAL RESPONSES

Impotence and unsustained or partial erections may occur as frequently as decreased libido. Here, too, neurotransmitter and/or hormonal abnormalities may be the basis. Occasionally the cause may be spinal cord injury (about 4 percent of head injuries are accompanied by spinal cord injuries). Less often the neurological deficit may be due to lumbosacral plexus[118] injuries, or peripheral neuropathy[119] (seen with some drug toxicities and for uncertain reasons in prolonged intensive care stays). Blood vessel injuries in the pelvic or genital regions are rarely the responsible factor. Injuries to the penis can cause impotence but we are unaware of reported cases with head injury. Many drugs produce impotence. Some of the chief potential causative substances in head trauma patients are:

- Tranquilizers
- Antidepressants
- Sedatives and hypnotics
- Antihypertensives
- Anticholinergic drugs[120]
- Antiseizure drugs
- Illicit drugs
- Alcohol
- Hormones (particularly progesterones)

Psychological factors are well-known causes of impotence: depression, anxiety, especially "performance anxiety" (fear of failure at sex), and distaste for the partner are examples of such factors. Less is known about the female equivalents of erection. It appears that the causes of impotence influence women's responses in similar fashion, but there is almost no information on this subject in brain injury literature.

Failure of ejaculation and retrograde ejaculation[121] are rare events after head injury. When they occur, spinal cord injury, lumbosacral plexus damage, or peripheral neuropathies are the usual causes. Rarely drugs like thioridazine (Mellaril, a tranquilizer) have caused difficulty with ejaculation. Premature ejaculation is a common functional problem unrelated to head injury or other physical disorders.

Total inability to achieve orgasm (anorgasmia[122]) despite arousal and erection is almost certainly an uncommon event after head injury. It might occur after localized damage to the nondominant temporal lobe, especially in deep injuries affecting the septal area of the limbic system. When anorgasmia is present, injury to the spinal cord or lumbosacral plexus, or peripheral nerve disorders should be investigated. Difficulty in achieving orgasm can be related to drugs (alcohol is a notable example). Extreme fatigability or pain can be the cause. The psychological factors previously mentioned must be considered. Inadequate or ineffective genital stimulation, with or without sensory deficits, can be responsible. Inadequate clitoral stimulation or insufficient pre-intercourse stimulation (foreplay) are possible causes of female anorgasmia.

Painful intercourse is often related to inadequate vaginal lubrication. Before or after menopausal vaginal changes due to hormonal deficiency, local infections or other gynecological[123] disorders are other likely causes. Men may experience painful intercourse due to injury or infections of the lower urinary tract or genitalia.

Vaginismus if the muscular constriction of the vagina, making penetration of the penis difficult. It is usually related to nonorganic factors.

## DISORDERS OF FERTILITY

Fertility problems are probably rare and chiefly due to hormonal deficiencies. Amenorrhea is extremely common immediately after brain injury, but customarily menstrual periods resume after four to six months. If amenorrhea persists beyond that period of time, hypothalamic-pituitary injury or dysfunction is a strong possibility. Injuries to the ovaries or testes are rarely associated with brain injury and do not appear to be a significant cause of infertility or hormone deficiency.

## DISORDERS OF MOBILITY

Mobility problems as the result of brain injury can interfere with sexual acts. Hemiplegia is often accompanied by spasticity, creating difficulties in transferring to and from bed, and in body positioning that interferes with penile-vaginal intercourse, graceful foreplay, and so forth. Apraxia may further complicate the picture, prohibiting willed movement upon request. Spasticity may increase with sexual excitement, causing injury to either partner, disturbing positioning and movement, and prohibiting effective lovemaking. Seizures may be precipitated by the deep and rapid breathing of sexual excitement, totally disrupting sexual activities, often to the dismay and fear of a sometimes unsuspecting partner. Ataxia and problems of equilibrium[124] can disturb positioning and transfers. Slow movement, rigidity, tremors, and other involuntary movements often impede motion, balance, and positioning. Limb deformities or amputations, particularly when tender or painful, can alter positioning and movement. Lack of interest in initiating activity or behavior, or apraxia may make a person totally passive during sexual activity. Deconditioning due to age, medical disorders, or prolonged inactivity can quickly exhaust a person who attempts sexual activity.

## DISORDERS OF SELF-CARE SKILLS

The activities of daily living called self-care skills are preparations for sexual activities and include emptying bowel or bladder, application of a contraceptive, undressing, hygienic care and grooming. These activities require planning and skill. Picture the head-injured person who is unkempt, childish, unable to plan ahead, and heedless of consequences. These self-care skills are unlikely to be of concern to him or her. Adequate limb function must be combined with capabilities of memory, perceptual ability, stepwise planning, pain-free motor and sensory control, and some degree of speed in processing. The factors mentioned in the section on mobility are equally applicable here. Both mobility and self-care deficiencies may be substituted for by an understanding, knowledgeable partner, or a trained attendant.

## DISORDERS OF SENSATION

Disorders of sensation resulting from brain injury have been described earlier. They often involve half of the body, rendering it insensitive to stimulation, including touch. In addition, the insensitive limbs may be incapable of providing stimulation to the partner. Unpleasant or painful sensations may also occur with brain injury, making the affected areas extremely uncomfortable to touch or pressure. Reduced or excessively sensitive sensation can result from associated spinal cord, plexus, nerve root, or peripheral nerve disorders. If the external genitalia[125] become insensitive, local touch stimulation may be ineffective in producing erection or vaginal lubrication. Peculiar or painful genital sensations may also interfere with sexual responses. A diminished or absent sense of position and movement creates difficulties in balance, posture, or movement during lovemaking. Loss of feelings of pain, temperature, or deep pressure removes warning systems that would alert the person to injury during sexual acts. Excessive force can produce soft tissue injuries or fractures to insensitive tissues. Lying in one position for prolonged periods can cause bed sores.

Loss of special senses such as sight, hearing, taste, and smell deprive people of stimuli that normally are an integral part of sexual arousal.

## DISORDERS OF COMMUNICATION AND ORAL FUNCTION

Communication and language skills applied to the sharing of desires and feelings between partners are often compromised. Aphasias as the result of dominant hemisphere injuries may be severe enough to drastically limit one's ability to speak, understand conversation, write, or read. Aphonia refers to loss of the voice. It usually is caused by disease or injury to the vocal cords, or paralysis of the muscles that control vocal cord movement.

Dysarthria is the difficulty in pronouncing words clearly. The condition is caused by weakness or paralysis of facial, throat, palatal, or tongue muscles, or uncoordination of those muscles due to cerebellar injuries. Dysarthria may accompany any of the movement disorders. It can be severe enough to make speech almost unintelligible as well as uncosmetic to eye and ear. Yet aphasias, aphonia, and dysarthria are often less disabling than the limited thoughts, words, or feelings displayed by the person with severe prefrontal lobe injury. Any of these problems in communication can be the source of extreme frustration for either partner. The inability to utter a sentimental phrase or to sing a favorite song may be eased by learning other ways of communicating. Perhaps the playing of a record, the exchange of a special look, or a mutually understood touch will convey the intended feelings.

Nonverbal communication may be meager or inappropriate. A perceptually impaired individual may misread the partner's facial expressions, intonation of voice, and body language. The ability to effectively convey feelings and desires by touch, caress, fondling, or a hug, may be lost or distorted. The monotonous, flat, seemingly emotionless voice of the perceptually impaired person can detract from the content of what is said.

Oral skills like kissing, sucking, and licking can be altered by the motor disorders mentioned in disorders of mobility. Cranial nerve injuries can further reduce these skills. Thus the repertoire of sexual activities may become restricted or distasteful and a source of further tensions to the couple.

## COSMETIC DISORDERS

Cosmetic disorders are often of great concern to the injured person. Head, facial, and body injuries may be disfiguring, and may require surgical reconstruction. Cranial nerve injuries can cause eye squints, weakness of facial muscles, drooping of one side of the face, or inability to close the eyelid. Oral and dental injuries may be unsightly. The anitseizure drug Dilantin produces overgrowth of the gums (gingiva[126]).

Reflex muscle spasms and other movement disorders may be distressing and even frightening to others. Extremities may shrivel (atrophy). Bony deformities due to complicated fractures or new bone growth (heterotopic bone[127]) in soft tissues around joints may be visible as well as painful. Scars of surgical incision or skin injuries are poorly accepted, especially on exposed parts of the body.

Medications like Dilantin or Dantrium, an antispasticity drug, can cause skin eruptions. Hormonal deficiencies can cause loss of secondary sex characteristics or abnormally early sexual development. Loss of bladder or bowel control can be humiliating and distressing to either partner.

Even mild cosmetic defects may produce extreme psychological discomfort for people whose personal and body images are otehwise disturbed by perceptual distortions and emotional distress. Whatever the severity or type of cosmetic defect, its impact on sexuality can be overwhelming. Shame, anxiety, and fear of rejection can sabotage all attempts at courtship or lovemaking.

## DISORDERS OF MENTAL FUNCTIONS

Our earlier description of brain syndromes included many of the mental disabilities resulting from brain injury. It is these remaining dysfunctions and their resultant social consequences that often have the most profound effects on sexuality. Some of these disorders are short-lived and disappear as recovery proceeds. Others may appear when the person returns to the community. Many disorders of mental functions can become more severe and progressive with time, due to the effects of secondary reactions of the person, family, treatment team, and community.

The behavioral, emotional, and personality changes described under frontal lobe syndromes are especially dramatic in the context of sexuality. Lack of control and poor judgment may take on specific sexual aspects. Brain-injured children and adults, often heedless of the consequences, are ready prey for sexual opportunists, or become the sexual aggressors who may indiscriminately verbally or physically abuse others. The lethargic, disinterested person is inevitably unrewarding as a sexual partner. So too is the selfish, insensitive individual. Sometimes the partner or spouse is embarrassed, frustrated, or angered to the point of rejection. Cognitive deficits and immature behavior may require the partner to become a caregiver rather than a mate. Emotional lability[128] and instability, as well as behavioral outbursts, may be set off by sexual activity, resulting in failure at attempted intercourse, additional frustration, and further explosive outbursts. The person with memory loss and perseveration may express unending repetitions of requests for sexual activity or repeated sex acts. He or she may forget that a sex act has just occurred or may be "stuck" on a certain behavior that is mindlessly repeated. The sexual partner can redirect the repetitious person to another activity, keep a logbook of activity as a reminder, or devise some other system with the partner to solve the problem. Openness and a sense of humor can reduce the stress of these situations. Pre-injury personality, behavior, or emotional disorders may worsen, although occasionally they are improved or disappear. Psychotic behavior sometimes results from brain injury. Depression may be organic, that is, directly the result of brain injury rather than due to realization of the effects of the injury. Certainly depression is a major cause of decreased libido and performance.

Drowsiness, confusion, disorientation, limited attention span, and distractibility may interfere with goal-directed behaviors including courtship, sensitive foreplay, and sexual acts. No doubt the many mental residuals of injury contribute to the decline in frequency of intercourse that is observed in the majority of brain-injured survivors who have available partners.

Perceptual losses can take many forms, as we have already seen. Any of the senses are subject to failure or distortion of interpretation and integration with other experiences. Most perceptual problems stem from the injuries to the parietal lobe on the nondominant side. We have illustrated some of the dramatic ways that perceptual disorders can disturb sexual function. For example, the inability to recognize a partner's body part by touch or even by sight. Perhaps a more subtle form is the inability to judge time, thus making the affected person unable to be on time for a date. Unless a partner is aware of the nature of such perceptual deficits, the situation is readily misunderstood, and the appropriate corrective measures are not attempted.

## SOCIAL DISORDERS

The social consequences of residual mental deficits can be isolation, inability to relate to others (especially the family), role reversals, dependency, difficulties with authorities, legal or criminal entanglements, drug abuse, inability to adapt to school or work, vagrancy, idleness, repeated institutional placements, and suicide. Maladaptive behaviors can lead to new injuries (often recurrent brain trauma) and medical complications such as uncontrolled late seizures, AIDS[129] (Acquired Immunodeficiency Syndrome), other sexually transmitted diseases, unwanted pregnancy, hepatitis, and blood infections. Children may become developmentally arrested and psychologically and socially immature. Estrangement from a spouse or partner may be more common than divorce. The toll on family and friends is often progressive with time. The injured person's social maladaptations often worsen, and consequently the reactions of the family intensify. Eventually the family can become physically and emotionally exhausted, financially depleted, and socially isolated.

# Psychological and Social Aspects of Sexuality before Injury

## DEVELOPMENTAL PERSPECTIVES

Due to the large number of young children, adolescents, and young adults who sustain head injuries, developmental issues are a major concern. Head injuries or neurological involvement frequently result in arrest or regression to a previous level of development. Times of transition from one period of development to another are especially sensitive to disruption as new behaviors and knowledge may not be well established. Of particular note is the struggle involved in merging from childhood to adulthood. This is a time of major physical, emotional, and cognitive change. The basic nature of the family and peer relationship becomes vastly altered and presents many new demands and pressures.

Interruption in the sexual-social development in a young child should not be minimized as skills are learned and built upon in order for future growth to occur. Both rehabilitation and family concerns often tend to focus on physical, behavioral, and academic changes and sometimes exclude social and sexual issues. A young child's attention to appropriate social interactions, especially involving language and behavior with family and peers, can be critical to later, more complex social development.

The family of a brain-injured child needs information about ''normal'' age-related behaviors and the development of social skills. Parents should be made aware of any gaps in the child's social skills. A number of excellent books on child development are available for these purposes. The preschool age child will not likely have access to a program directly relating to brain injury issues. Therefore, parents may have to carefully select a preschool program that is fairly well structured and yet allows for changes in approach as the child recovers. Additionally, the program should emphasize learning social skills. Frequent behavioral problems after injury are poor attention, hyperactivity, impulsivity, and aggressiveness.

During this period, parents should provide their children with age-appropriate sexual education. If the child has learning problems, parents must ensure that the material is presented in such a way that the child has a clear and correct grasp of the subject. There are a number of books available which can assist parents in discussing sexual issues with their children. A parent can best appreciate the child's current knowledge or misunderstandings by having open discussions with him or her from time to time.

A child's dependence on parents is normal; however, after injury that dependence can increase and extend over time. Issues of dependence and independence are especially difficult under these circumstances. Impulsivity and poor judgment can result in increased need for supervision. Apathetic or listless behavior may require close parental structuring of the child's activity. With either of these extremes, parents may be uncertain as the degree of supervision and structure that is indicated. Thus they require much support and assistance in dealing with these matters. Separation from parents and formulation of a self-identity relates directly to later issues of appropriate socialization and sexuality. Parents can obtain information on behavior management techniques through local parent support organizations or classes offered at community colleges. A psychologist can assist in setting up behavior management programs that the parents and school can then implement. A thorough understanding of pre-injury development and individual personality factors is essential to fill the particular needs of each child.

The older child (5 to 10 years) deals with formulation of values and attitudes involving social-sexual development. Furthermore, this is a time when more formal knowledge is sought. Again, structured social skills training is important with the addition of "factual" education. The child's increasing awareness of how he or she is perceived by friends is a normal development occurring during this age period. Disruption of normal social interactions without suitable help can greatly affect the following stage of adolescence. Social skills which are the basis of later teenage dating may be inadequate and result in rejection and isolation. After head injury, this age group may have difficulty with awareness of social boundaries and may behave in a manner which results in the loss of peer relationships. These issues require a direct program of reeducation involving the child, school environment, and family. Parents should communicate closely with the school and work directly with the teacher in this process. The teacher will need help in understanding the basis of behavior problems.

In fact, it is much easier to head off problems which are predictable in adolescence by dealing with them during this earlier, calmer, developmental stage. Help from a therapist who can assist the child and parents in changing undesirable behaviors or poor self-image can forestall future difficulties. Self-esteem can be enhanced through sports, social activities, counseling, and skills training. Deficient self-esteem can lead to many emotional problems and poor relationships with friends, family, and teachers. The child may withdraw from social interaction or act out in search of additional attention. These behaviors can persist as lifelong patterns.

Injury during the adolescent period of development often results in a wide range of behaviors both childlike and experimental in nature. This is an age when experimenting is typical. There is a limited understanding and awareness of responsibilities and consequences of new behavior. Additionally, this age group is often more open to information and influence from peers and the media rather than from adults. Due to the controversy in this country surrounding the systematic provision of sex education there is little that can be counted on as factual information. Families differ greatly in their approaches to educating their children about sexual issues. Sexual experiences within the same age group can be extremely varied. This is especially true of adolescents. A young adult can range from being sexually ignorant and unexperienced to being knowledgeable and very experienced. The adolescent is breaking away from the family and beginning to establish a self-identity.

During this stage of development, the adolescent is establishing patterns of man/woman relationships that can be continued throughout life. Learning how to express feelings of caring and closeness is a complicated process and is vulnerable to many influences. Adolescents tend to be acutely aware of appearances. Therefore, alteration of physical appearance can be devastating to self-esteem and self-concept during this stage. Peer counseling and groups offering education and emotional support can be effective. Resources like Planned Parenthood are available to provide information and help with birth control. Parents may need to assume a directive role in this area. Family counseling and education are often necessary for this age group, as the strains on the family can be enormous. Under normal circumstances parents of adolescents are confronted with many difficult issues.

When the adolescent has a brain injury the parents may be faced with a nightmare. Conflicts over boundary setting are more likely to occur with close parental supervision. In many cases, friends must be carefully screened and close tabs must be kept on the teenager's moment-to-moment whereabouts and activities. Teenage girls are particularly vulnerable to sexual advances and abuse. Exposure to pregnancy and sexually transmitted diseases are a concern that parents must confront. Some parents may choose to establish the use of birth control methods. This issue can be the cause of conflict between the parents themselves, as well as between parents and child.

The question of voluntary versus involuntary birth control is an especially difficult matter. Each family must find its own answer after obtaining adequate information and counseling from such sources as a counselor, physician, lawyer, and the family's rabbi or minister.

A developmental perspective has merit when examining premorbid adult functioning. Generalizations cannot be made about sexual-social skills of development. A careful analysis of pre-injury social and sexual history is essential. Unresolved developmental issues may be present and should be addressed. A stable sex role relies upon experiences, habits, and expectations in pursuing and maintaining intimate relationships. Furthermore, these practices and expectations are reflections of the beliefs and value systems that are part of the person. Problems in these areas may have existed prior to the injury. Certainly after head injury, with the major stress placed on the family system, any previously existing problems will be exaggerated.

Many brain-injured persons have pre-injury histories of poor relationships with both their own family and peers. Sexual preference prior to injury may not have been established. Previous sexual experiences may have been deviant as a result of abuse, neglect, incest, or rape. Assumptions about these sensitive subjects should not be made without adequate information that will provide the basis for treatment decisions. Families can help provide this information. Problems that existed prior to injury generally do not improve and may be compounded by the multitude of additional physical, cognitive, emotional, and behavioral deficits related to the head injury.

## OTHER SIGNIFICANT BEFORE-INJURY FACTORS

Before-injury factors play a significant role in the occurrence of head injuries. These factors have further implications in predicting the types of sexual difficulties that ensue.

Twice as many males suffer brain injury as do females. Young people are extremely vulnerable. Persons in the age range of 15 to 29 years are at high risk of injury, with those between 15 and 19 years at greatest risk.

Alcohol abuse is receiving increasing attention as a factor in accidents resulting in head injury. A recent review of statistics in the United States pointed out that of those 100,000 people who annually die in accidents, 70 percent die of head injury. The University of Virginia Department of Motor Vehicle Study documented that 86 percent of all accident victims with head injury had alcohol in their blood at the time of injury. About half of those people were legally intoxicated.

Emotional and behavioral problems that existed before injury can strongly influence sexual behavior after injury. Emotional instability, depression, and antisocial characteristics are associated with poor sexual adjustment prior to head injury. A frequently identifiable symptom of depression is decreased sexual desire and interest. Emotional instability invariably is associated with social and relationship problems.

Individuals with antisocial tendencies have difficulty forming emotional bonds and often see a sexual partner as someone to be used for self-gratification and have little or no consideration for the partner. Generally, these people are not improved by the injury. Their behaviors may be less well controlled and more apparent to others.

In summary, a number of pre-injury factors have been noted. Sex, marital status, alcohol use, and behavioral and emotional factors have been identified as major issues. Family, legal, vocational, and peer problems are all interrelated and contribute to an increased likelihood of breakdown in social and sexual relationships. A thorough understanding of all of these areas is necessary to the appreciation of the nature of problems that become more severe or frequent after head injury.

The cognitive problems outlined previously can affect sexual and social functioning even in cases of mild head injury. In fact, friends and family may be less understanding and supportive because the individual looks "fine." Education of the person, family, and significant others can make the difference between the survival or failure of an important supportive relationship. Families can seek information and support to assist in adapting to the many changes occurring after injury. Support groups can be helpful in exploring these issues. All concerned should appreciate that eventual improvement is the rule. Headaches and impotency often are a problem after a mild head injury and usually disappear over time. In the meantime, these problems may be responsive to medical treatment. Emotional problems can later appear if proper education and counseling is not provided in these situations.

Regardless of the type and severity of injury, the diverse pre-injury life-styles, family interrelationships, beliefs, and sexual practices must be recognized as contributing factors to postinjury sexual function. Each family has its own ways of showing love and caring for one another. Every person's "way" needs to be recognized and accepted, provided that it does not infringe on the rights and welfare of others.

# Psychological and Social Aspects of Sexuality after Injury

## REACTIONS OF BRAIN-INJURED PERSONS

The reactions of the brain-injured individual are an evolving process. As self-awareness increases, the person proceeds through a number of emotional and behavioral reactions. Behavior that occurred in the early stages of recovery may have resulted in changed roles with spouse and significant others. Such role alterations may produce a continuation of childlike dependence, and a parent-child rather than adult-spouse relationship.

Confusion is prevalent in earlier stages of recovery. This confusion can lead to blurred sexual identity.[130] Sexual overtures to a person of the same sex can be seen in individuals who did not previously evidence this behavior. Teenagers may revert to earlier experimental homosexual activities. As the early dependence and confusion improve, the family and significant others should attempt to progressively return to pre-injury ways of relating, emphasizing the encouragement of independence and decision making.

Prolonged removal from the community can result in little or no opportunity to have appropriate sexual contact. The treatment team or family may view the person as asexual or childlike. These factors adversely affect his or her sexual self-perception. Attention to these matters is essential and may have a long-term effect on a person's ability to reestablish relationships. Opportunity for sexual contact must be offered without undue pressure. Performance anxiety may be present for the individual as well as the spouse or significant other, and should be addressed. Before sexual activity resumes, discussion of these fears with both partners can considerably ease concerns. Depression and poor self-esteem, as well as reaction to prolonged stress, which are so much a part of the recovery process, may themselves result in decreased sex drive.

Return to community life presents new situations that lack the degree of structure and control created in the hospital or rehabilitation center environment. The adaptive and other functional skills of the recovering person can be sorely tested. Failures may occur. The reality of the remaining dysfunctions may now be more fully appreciated by the survivor as well as those who surround him or her. Frustration, embarrassment, anger, despondency, and hopelessness are common feelings. Some survivors may have no insight into their limitations and blithely attempt to resume their former activities, including work and driving. Other responsible parties, often family and friends, may be forced to intervene, creating restrictions that the survivor does not understand or tolerate. Frequently family members receive the brunt of the person's anger, confusion, and sense of loss.

Isolation and loneliness may progressively increase. The recovering person frequently feels rejected and unworthy because of the attitudes and behaviors of others. Mounting feelings of alienation from partner, family, health care team, and society may follow. Irritability, impatience, and hostility toward others can result in acting out to the point of violence. Conversely, the survivor can become increasingly withdrawn and indifferent. Occasionally the despondent, hopeless person may consider or attempt suicide.

## REACTIONS OF THE PARTNER AND FAMILY

The reactions of the partner and family may take many forms. The caretaker, breadwinner role of the partner can be all-consuming. Earlier hope of recovery can give way to resignation, the sense of entrapment, and isolation. The massive responsibilities heaped upon the partner can lead to anxiety, fear, loneliness, depression, guilt, anger, and frustration. Fear may specifically relate to the concern that sexual activity may somehow injure the disabled partner. Sexual desire and interest may wane, and be replaced, on occasion, by a feeling of disinterest or distaste for the injured person. Sexual interest may turn to another person. The psychological stresses inherent in the situation can lead to physical symptoms such as fatigue, headaches, gastrointestinal problems, and so forth. It seems likely that sexual dysfunctions of the healthy partner are as frequent as those of the individual with injury.

Indeed no member of the survivor's immediate family is unscathed. Many of the reactions just described also occur in other members. Children of the survivor may lose a male or female role model as well as a parent. Their own role with that former parent may revert to that of the adult tending a child. The child may exhibit delayed psychosocial development, sexual identity confusion, regressive behavior, or other types of acting out. Abuse by peers may occur. Self-concept and self-esteem may suffer as much as those of the disabled parent. Thus the suffering of the child becomes part of the suffering of the parents. All family members may share the embarrassment, guilt, estrangement, and fatigue of the survivor; feelings that can intensify over time. Social isolation and ostracism directed at the family can be even more severe than that directed at the injured person. Often friends have difficulty understanding the nature of the family's duress, and bluntly indicate that they do not want to hear about "the problem" anymore. Stressful reactions of family members are most readily dealt with by anticipation, prevention, or early management. In some communities support groups are offered for children with disabled siblings or parents. Local community information services can help in locating these resources. Counseling is another avenue of support, enabling the family to better understand their own emotional responses as well as those of the community. Support groups for family members are often helpful in combating feelings of stress and isolation.

## REACTIONS OF THE TREATMENT TEAM

The professional staff is susceptible to some of these same reactions. Pity, oversolicitousness, and treating the person as a child are difficult to avoid. At the other extreme, callousness, indifference, and anger can surface. Frustration and burnout are often experienced. The staff may feel insecure and uncomfortable to the point of avoiding the issues of sexuality. Professionals may treat the survivor as an asexual person. Normal sexual urges may be viewed as abnormal or excessive in the hospital or residential setting. On the other hand, there can be sexual attraction or an intimate relationship with the survivor. The staff can constructively identify problems of the patient such as inaccessibility to sexual opportunities or lack of education and experience. Or the team will recognize its own limitations such as inadequate education and training, institutional restrictions, and proceed to deal with these problems.

This type of team critique is not always addressed in rehabilitation programs. It is often difficult for staff to define appropriate emotional boundaries for themselves. Unfortunately, unethical and abusive behaviors toward disabled children are not unheard of. Clear guidelines and careful supervision are needed in any program serving adults or children with disabilities.

## REACTIONS OF THE COMMUNITY

Community reactions may echo family and staff reactions. Rejection, ridicule, ostracism, and punishment may evolve out of ignorance and misunderstanding. Legal proceedings, commitment to mental institutions, or arrests, are frequent societal responses to maladaptive behaviors. So too are the responses of pity, fostering of overdependence, and treating the person like a child. These attitudes can be addressed by all parties involved. Survivors, family members, and professionals must constantly educate the public. Opportunities to speak to public groups and children should not be missed. Acting and speaking for one's self is the strongest source of empowerment. Appropriate anger should be expressed so that long-term changes in unjust attitudes and behaviors can occur. Involvement with state head injury foundation societies is an effective way to channel educational and political efforts.

# Evaluation

## HISTORY

How can sexuality and sexual function be evaluated? The way to begin is with a comprehensive sexual and health history taken by a health care professional who is knowledgeable about both sexuality and brain injury. The history may not be obtainable for the brain-injured person who has profound memory loss, other cognitive deficits, or a severe communication disorder. In those instances a spouse, partner, or family member can provide historical information, or verify, add to, and correct the information provided by the subject. When attention span and concentration are limited, the history can be obtained over several or more sessions. The preinjury history is vital. A full understanding of medical aspects is as essential as appreciation of psychosocial data. An available partner can provide further information, offer insights concerning the partner and the relationship, and furnish details concerning his or her own sexual function. Sexual problems of the partner may contribute to those of the subject, and vice versa.

## PHYSICAL EXAMINATION

Following the history, a physical examination is performed. The examination should be thorough, with particular attention to the nervous, musculoskeletal, hormonal, peripheral blood vessel, reproductive, and urinary systems.

An extension of the physical examination is the functional assessment provided by the rehabilitation team. The customary evaluations by team members include assessments of mobility, self-care skills, communications and oral functions; psychological testing, and a social inventory. During or after a comprehensive hospital rehabilitation program, these functional evaluations can be extended to focus specifically on their relationship to sexuality. For example, the mobility assessment can include observations about transfers, positioning, and movement as they relate to sexual activities.

## OTHER STUDIES

Depending upon the results of the history and physical examination, laboratory studies can be requested to confirm the diagnostic impressions of any identified sexual dysfunctions.

Some of these laboratory assessments have become a highly specialized set of examinations that may not be readily available in every hospital or clinic setting. Specialty clinics in sexuality or impotence have burgeoned in an effort to fully evaluate and comprehensively treat sexual dysfunctions. However, it may be necessary to provide the history, physical examination, and functional assessments before referral to the specialty clinic if the clinical professional staff is not geared to the complexities of physical and psychosocial disabilities ensuing from brain injury and its associated conditions. A thorough explanation of the purpose and nature of each of these assessments is essential, as is a clear interpretation of the result of the studies and recommendations for treatment.

# Management

## PRINCIPLES OF INTERDISCIPLINARY CARE

Effective treatment follows the comprehensive assessment, interpretation of that assessment, and full disclosure and explanation of the findings to the person, partner, or family. As a rule, management involves the utilization of many types of treatment. The systems of treatment include medical, functional (training and education of living skills), and supportive methods. We do not believe that treatment should await the traditional "cues" of readiness given by the disabled person or family. The management process is continuous and progressive, beginning in the hospital setting soon after injury. Ideally, it is a process that the rehabilitation team routinely undertakes as part of a total plan of restoration. Thus all professional disciplines share concern and responsibility for sexual rehabilitation. This basic philosophy has increasingly become a reality in many rehabilitation programs, but is not a universal practice. Staff education and training in sexuality and sexual function is a prerequisite for open and informed management. Often the team will use a system termed the PLISSIT model (Table 11). PLISSIT represents four levels of dealing with sexual concerns by professionals on a health care team. "P" symbolizes *permission*: giving approval for a patient or family to discuss sexual matters. "LI" indicates *limited information*: providing the information that a professional is competent and comfortable with giving. "SS" stands for *specific suggestions*: offering more

**Table 11**

## THE PLISSIT MODEL FOR ADDRESSING PATIENTS' SEXUAL CONCERNS

| | | |
|---|---|---|
| P | Permission | Rehabilitation team members should let the patient and family know that it is all right to be concerned about sexual matters and encourage open discussions. |
| LI | Limited information | Team members can help clear up misconceptions and ease anxieties by imparting what they know. Team members can use diagrams, anatomical information, or statistics to help the patient understand, but should only stick to what they know and are comfortable talking about. |
| SS | Specific suggestions | At this level of intervention, the rehabilitation team member proposes a specific course of action such as joining a support group, doing certain exercises, or investigating sexual aids. |
| IT | Intensive therapy | When the client's sexual concerns are not met by permission to discuss, limited information, or specific suggestions, the rehabilitation team member should help the client find the necessary expert help. |

detailed counsel and recommendations to the patient and family. "IT" represents *intensive therapy*: highly specialized and often continuing counsel and related treatment by experts in sexual therapy. These four levels of therapy allow professionals of every discipline and level of training to participate in some area of sexual rehabilitation just as they do with any other sphere of function of the disabled person. Sexual training can be an extension, a further application, of knowledge and skills taught to patient and family by each discipline. Let us look at some examples of how this works.

Physical therapists, occupational therapists, and rehabilitation nurses can extend mobility and self-care training to include preparation for, and participation in, sexual activity. As part of preparation, hygienic and cosmetic aspects such as skin and mouth care and bowel and bladder emptying may need attention. The ability to remember and properly use contraceptive devices must be tested. Dressing and undressing may require further instruction and modification in clothing. Unwilled movement disorders may be controlled by relaxation, biofeedback, positional changes, proper timing of medicines, and other methods. Painful, stiff limbs may be responsive to heat, gentle stretching, and pain medication taken shortly before planned activity. Instruction to patient and partner in transfers, motor skills in preparing for and proceeding with sexual activity, helpful positions to assume, and the type of bed mattress or other surface are additional details where the therapist's input is beneficial. Proper positioning and adequate support can reduce drooling, muscle spasm, and pain, while enhancing comfort, movement, access to the partner, balance, and sensitivity to touch. Occupational therapists can provide sensory and perceptual retraining, identifying areas of intact sensation for purposes of touch and other pleasurable, exciting stimuli. They may recommend adaptive aids[131] to improve upper extremity function or modifications of the environment. Training patient and partner in the use of a vibrator or dildo[132] (penis-shaped devices) may begin with the therapist (Fig. 21).

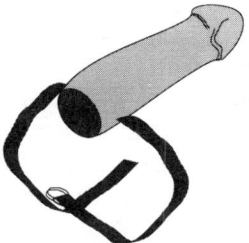

**A** Rigid cover of
penis with strap

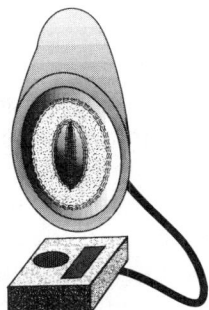

**B** Artificial vagina with
electrical vibrator

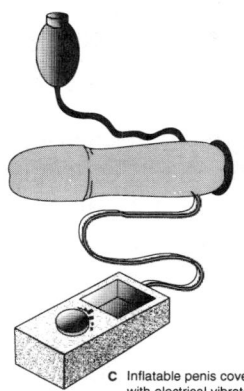

**C** Inflatable penis cover
with electrical vibrator

**Figure 21.** Examples of sexual aids. (A) Rigid penis cover with strap. (B) Artificial vagina with electrical vibrator. (C) Inflatable penis cover with electrical vibrator.

Therapeutic exercises and physical agents (physical modalities[133]) that are customarily utilized by physical and occupational therapists may have specific applications to sexual functions. Many of these techniques can be taught to the brain-injured person or partner for use at home. Obviously, this is a sensitive area for therapists and their clients. Therapists who are uncomfortable in this role may refer the client and partner to a colleague who is more at ease in this area.

We have mentioned the value of heat and stretching in relieving certain types of pain. Biofeedback[134] and electrical stimulation are also of potential value in pain management. Deconditioned patients will benefit from strengthening and endurance exercises which can lead to decreased fatigability and improved positioning capabilities during sexual activity. Training in motor control and speed, coordination, and balance can improve sexual motor performance. Some contracture[135] deformities will benefit from combinations of heating and sustained stretching as by progressive casting or splinting. A difficult or uncosmetic gait may be altered by ambulation training with an inconspicuous plastic short leg brace.

Speech pathologists, occupational therapists, and psychologists are involved with cognitive training.[136] The training program can be constructed to encompass many aspects of sexuality. Early body orientation can include identification of sexual organs, which are often among the first body parts to be self-discovered upon arousal from coma. The provision of sexual information should proceed in a progressive fashion and be geared to changing levels of attention, memory, and other mental abilities. Memory deficits relating to sexual activities can be managed by use of a daily ledger or audio tape recording which includes notations of when menstrual periods and sexual acts have occurred as well as a check list of preparatory activities for sex.

Treatment of emotional and behavioral problems can be directed specifically at sexual concerns. Under the psychologist's direction, the rehabilitation team can construct programs to modify undesirable, inappropriate behaviors such as exposure, masturbation, and foul language. Systematic rewards can be given for desirable, appropriate behaviors. Social attention, special privileges, favorite recreational activities, and rest are examples of the inducements (positive reinforcements) that help maintain trouble-free behaviors. The undesirable behaviors are either totally ignored and unrewarded, or in some instances, immediately followed by a period of isolation in a quiet room (time out). These and other behavioral methods have proven to be quite successful, in many cases, in dealing with difficult, otherwise unyielding sexual behaviors. In addition, the psychologist often coordinates the sexual education and counseling programs for patients, partners, couples, or groups. Specific sexual therapy is another area of expertise of many psychologists.

The speech pathologist's role in communication and language training can include verbal and nonverbal expressions of affection, love, and desire. The discreetness and appropriateness of such communication usually demands attention. A limiting factor in training may be the severity of intellectual deficits and associated limitations in thought and speech. The speech pathologist can assist in expanding the repertoire of phrases available to the survivor. Aphasic patients may learn to substitute gestures and other nonverbal forms of communication for speech. Some patients can be trained to use augmentative communications devices,[137] electronic devices that "speak" or "write" for them. Perceptually disturbed patients may benefit from instruction in recognizing the more subtle aspects of speech and of nonverbal cues. Problems of lip and tongue control and drooling are also within the area of expertise of the speech pathologist.

The team, particularly the recreational therapist, occupational therapist, social worker, and psychologist, can organize social skills training that will enhance confidence, self-image, and ease in communicating with others. Such training is frequently a major focus of the program, since social skills are so often a problem area, even after mild brain injury. Community and leisure skills should be directed toward dating activities and resuming and building social contacts.

In the hospital or any other setting, the brain-injured patient needs privacy to experiment and practice the more specific and intimate techniques described above, communicate with the partner, and discuss and inquire about sexuality. Most hospital rehabilitation programs provide a room or suite on or near the nursing unit that allows privacy. Usually the rehabilitation nurse is the ultimate coordinator of newly acquired skills and information, assuring that what has been achieved in therapies is actually applied on the nursing unit. Therefore, the nurse can serve patient and partner as the trainer in the private room. Demonstrations of sexual anatomy and positional variations can be simplified by the use of anatomical models and flexible dolls. Activities may be assigned by the trainer who leaves the room, then later reviews the assignment with the person or couple. What if there is no partner to share in the education, training, and practice of sexual functioning? We do not recommend the use of sexual surrogates (substitute sexual partners) as a component of rehabilitation programs. The matter of sexual surrogates involves controversial legal and ethical issues. However, social surrogates such as persons who act as "dates" or social companions are an acceptable and useful part of the training program.

An overview of rehabilitation team member roles and functions is provided in Table 12. What if the brain-injured person has not had the opportunity for such comprehensive sexual training by a team of rehabilitation professionals? What can the family or partner do in the home setting? The following two case reports illustrate approaches in managing some frequently occurring problems.

## Table 12

## REHABILITATION TEAM MEMBERS: ROLES AND FUNCTIONS

| *Who Am I?* | *What Do I Do?* |
| --- | --- |
| Physiatrist | Primary care physician on the rehabilitation hospital service. Medical director of the rehabilitation team. Usually coordinates the rehabilitation team program. |
| Social worker | Evaluate and counsel regarding social functions and adjustment of patient and family. Provide information on resources available to person and family. Coordinate hospital discharge planning and reentry into community. |
| Rehabilitation nurse | Coordinate training on the rehabilitation bed unit. Evaluate and manage bowel and bladder habits and skin care. Educate person and family in health care and medications. |
| Occupational therapist | Train in self-care skills, household, community, and work skills. Assist in cognitive training and socialization. Train in upper limb functions, and sensory and perceptual training. Provide adaptive aids and alterations to home. |
| Physical therapist | Provide therapeutic exercises to improve muscle control, coordination, strength, endurance, movement, and posture control. Provide training in mobility skills: transfers, walking, and so forth. Evaluate physical environment of home. |

*(continued)*

**Table 12**

## REHABILITATION TEAM MEMBERS: ROLES AND FUNCTIONS (*Continued*)

| *Who Am I?* | *What Do I Do?* |
| --- | --- |
| Speech-language pathologist | Evaluate and treat disorders of speech, language, and communications such as aphonia, dysarthria, aphasia, and aprosody. Assist in cognitive training. Evaluate and treat swallowing disorders and drooling. |
| Rehabilitation psychologist | Neuropsychological testing and interpretation. Coordinate cognitive retraining and behavior training. Evaluate and treat emotional problems. Provide psychological counseling of patient, family, groups, and sex and marital counseling. |
| Dietitian | Study and treat nutritional disorders. Provide dietary recommendations for medical disorders. Provide consultation on special feeding problems such as formulas for nasogastric tube feedings, gastrostomy feedings, and so forth. |
| Prosthetist, orthotist | Make and fit artificial limbs (prosthetist). Make and fit braces (orthotist). |
| Vocational counselor | Evaluate person for work potential. Counsel on further educational or work training requirements. Coordinate training of work skills. Coordinate job placement and follow-up after placement. |
| Recreational therapist | Evaluate and coordinate training in recreation and leisure skills. Coordinate rehabilitation service recreational programs. Participate in |

**Table 12**

**REHABILITATION TEAM MEMBERS: ROLES AND
FUNCTIONS** (*Continued*)

| Who Am I? | What Do I Do? |
| --- | --- |
|  | social skills and interpersonal skills training. |
| Teacher | Teach academic subjects. Provide special education based on cognitive deficits and deficits in basic academic skills that are disclosed by psychological, communications, language, and academic achievement tests. |

A teenage boy is recovering from left and right sided pre-frontal lobe injuries sustained in an auto accident. Six months after injury, he lives at home with his parents and an older teenage brother. The lad is alert, fully oriented, and has regained good memory and most other mental capacities. However, he is impulsive and sometimes uninhibited. Neighbors have brought to the family's attention several incidents in which the boy has publicly displayed his penis and masturbated. How should the family deal with this behavior?

The parents and brother can, in a calm, deliberate manner, devise a behavior program that will have several goals: (1) to progressively reduce and then stop the undesirable public behaviors—exhibiting his genitals and masturbating, (2) to provide the opportunity for masturbation in an appropriate private place at home—his room, (3) to teach substitute public behaviors and establish a reward system for ensuring their increasing frequency of occurrence.

The family can decide on the details of a program by working out some strategies to achieve each of these three goals. For example, the first goal could be addressed by deciding that the boy would be accompanied by a member of the family on all public outings for a given period of time. If inappropriate behaviors occur, the boy would promptly be escorted home and "grounded" from further outings for a period of time such as the next 24 hours. If the undesirable behaviors occur indoors, the lad would be placed in an unoccupied "quiet room" for a period of approximately 15 minutes. These actions would be carried out without scolding or involved discussion. As part of the entire program, these actions would be discussed with the boy and approved of by him before the program begins.

The second goal would be addressed by the family's assurance that the boy would have the opportunity to retire to his room at any time he wished to masturbate. He should be reassured that masturbation is a normal behavior and that there are no ill effects from it. Usually it is not necessary to mention that excessively frequent, prolonged, or vigorous masturbation might cause local irritation or injury.

The third goal could be fulfilled by devising a system that rewards appropriate public behaviors immediately after each public venture. For instance, after returning home from an outing, the supervising family member, and any others if present, would offer sincere praise and social attention to the boy. Another immediate reward might be the payment of tokens (such as poker chips) that can be applied toward a desirable activity such as a movie. After a sufficient number of tokens are earned (5 chips = a movie) he is rewarded by being allowed to perform the desired activity. The exact nature of the rewards can often be worked out during the pre-program discussion with the boy. His active participation and approval of the program, even if he does not like every last detail, will help ensure success.

The other key point in planning for the third goal is to teach the boy acceptable behaviors to substitute for the undesirable ones. For example, he could be taught to immediately respond to the urge to display his penis. He could say to himself, "No! I won't do that. I will instead talk to my family member about where we are going and what we will be doing when we get there." Then he would proceed to talk, as he had planned. The boy would discuss the reasons for doing this, and would rehearse it at regular intervals with the family, including any occasions when the undesirable behaviors occur.

With the progressive improvement of the undesired behaviors, supervision can be reduced and eventually withdrawn entirely. The reward system can be extended to allow greater intervals of time between rewards. If one reward system is not effective, another set of rewards should be tried. The frequency of both desired and undesired behaviors should be closely monitored and recorded to insure that changes are truly occurring.

---

A 28-year-old woman returns to her husband and two young children after recuperating from a severe closed head injury that resulted from an auto accident. She has been hospitalized for nearly five months, including a 10 week stay in a rehabilitation program. Although she has improved greatly since the original injuries (including several fractures—one of the left lower leg and one of the pelvis), she remains with a right hemiparesis. Also, she has word-finding difficulties, problems with recent memory, and feels anxious about resuming responsibilities as a wife and mother. Although she and her husband have received instruction regarding sexuality, they are concerned about resuming sexual relations. Neither wants another child at this time. She does not feel very interested in sex, but wants to be able to please her husband. He is eager to resume their previously satisfying sexual relationship, but is concerned that she is still recovering from major injuries, has some difficulty in maneuvering because of the right-sided weakness, and is still sore at the sites of her fractures. He is fearful that he may cause her more pain on attempted intercourse. Both have misgivings about how attractive they will be to one another as they resume their physical intimacy. How can they begin again?

First, they can obtain medical advice about choosing a contraceptive. The physician should be supplied with medical information that will help to determine the best method. The physician should know that the woman has no effective use of her right hand, and that she has recent memory deficits. Rather than prescribe a diaphragm or cyclic hormone pills, the physician might recommend a method such as a long-acting hormone implanted under the skin.

Before attempting intercourse or other sexual activity, the couple can practice ways of becoming physically comfortable with one another. At a time of privacy and quiet, they can explore ways of expressing love and affection for one another without the pressure of feeling the need to proceed to a specific sexual activiity. This understanding can be discussed and agreed upon beforehand. Any means of expression can be practiced: talking, touching, massage, hugging, reading aloud, listening to music, or whatever promises to be pleasurable for both people. They can practice letting each other know what feels comfortable and pleasurable, and what does not. The couple can apply the techniques they learned from the rehabilitation program to aid in clearly communicating their feelings, despite her language problem. After gaining confidence with these activities, the couple can explore different positions that might be used during sexual activities. The wife might feel more stable and comfortable with pillows supporting her back and pelvis while lying partially on one side. She could try lying more toward her right side to provide free use of her left-sided limbs. She might try lying on her abdomen, perhaps with pillows supporting the abdomen and the right arm. The couple should feel free to try any position that is comfortable for both people and permits the intended activity to occur.

Now the couple can proceed to specific sexual activities. They can explore various parts of each other's body to learn whether previous means of arousal still work. The husband should be especially patient in this foreplay. If his wife is not responsive to the activity, foreplay can be sustained for a longer period of time. She may guide him toward more effective stimulation, for example, placing his hand in a more advantageous position for effective stimulation of the clitoris. The best cue that she is being aroused is the presence of increased vaginal wetness. What if vaginal secretion remains scant? Additional methods of stimulation may prove helpful. For those couples who find it comfortable and acceptable, oral stimulation may work. Others may use an electrical vibrator as a stimulator to the genital organs, particularly the clitoris, or other parts of the body. Vibrators may be purchased in drugstores or "adult" stores. The latter establishments are resources for many forms of stimulation that may be helpful in arousal. Erotic audiovisual aids, literature, and equipment such as vibrators and penile or vaginal-shaped devices are among the available items (Fig. 21). Models of the genital organs are useful in reviewing the anatomy of the area. If inadequate vaginal lubrication persists, a water-soluble lubricant like K-Y Jelly (available at drugstores) can be applied to the vagina or penis to ease penetration.

Because of his anxieties, the husband may also be slow to arouse, or experience temporary impotence. The same principles of unpressured practice of preliminaries, effective ways to stimulate one another, and patience are applicable. The couple should agree at the start that they do not have to have "success" the first or second time they try. They should allow themselves to get lost in expressing and feeling love for one another; they should forget about performance.

Finally, the couple should agree on ways to share responsibilities for the care of home and children. He has already addressed many of these problems in her absence. Now she must be allowed to regain her role, according to her capabilities, as homemaker, wife, and mother. At the same time, care must be taken that these responsibilities are not suddenly dumped upon her. The children must learn who their mother is, and what their father's role will now be. The reintegration of the woman into the family unit will certainly be reflected in her sexual life. As she regains skill and confidence in herself as mother, wife, and homemaker, she will regain skill and confidence as lover.

## EARLY HOSPITAL CARE

The earliest team focus is on support, counseling, and education of spouse, partner, or family in the intensive care unit (ICU). At first these efforts are broad in scope, aimed at providing and interpreting current medical information, answering questions, providing emotional support, identifying and enlisting immediate resources, and allowing for opportunities of expression of love and care for the stricken patient. These expressions often fall victim to the family's preoccupation with the critical medical situation and the lack of privacy. With the approval and training of the ICU nursing staff, the family can begin to participate in some aspects of bedside care, a laying on of loving hands. Moments of privacy should be permitted, if possible. The family should be encouraged to speak to the patient and to display affection, understanding that he or she may or may not be capable of appreciating what is said or done. Once survival seems assured, the family can be instructed on what might be expected as recovery proceeds. More specific information relating to sexuality can be initiated. Agitation can be described with the explanation that as speech is regained, cursing, vulgarity, and sexual references may be voiced. Even a Victorian upbringing does not preclude such outbursts, although in such a case, these behaviors will not likely persist. The survivor's early semipurposeful or purposeful exploration of his or her body may be directed to the genitalia. Such self-stimulation is part of the waking process. It need not be prevented. Rather, privacy and safety should be provided, along with reassurance to the family. The survivor's exploration of others can be similarly focused, without regard for whom the object happens to be. The distress of shock, shame, or guilt can be averted or lessened by sensitive discussions of these expected behaviors and how to deal with them. Other uninhibited behaviors such as exposure, public masturbation, and inappropriate solicitation can likewise be anticipated and managed by behavior techniques such as reinforcing more desirable activities and ignoring the inappropriate ones. These techniques require careful planning, consistency, and close communication among all people involved if success is to be achieved.

## LATER HOSPITAL CARE

As the patient recovers from early confusion, agitation, and disorientation, and graduates from the posttraumatic amnesic state (inability to remember events from the time of the accident onward), the rehabilitation team can progressively educate and train the person and family according to the functional model described earlier. Behavioral training can be expanded to teach more complex and suitable interpersonal and social skills. The person may be amenable to learning and reviewing basic sexual information related to his or her disability. Persistent undesirable behaviors may require momentary isolation (time out), immediate identification of the behavior in question (why it is undesirable), demonstration of a suitable substitute behavior (why it is desirable), and then the practice of that suitable behavior. An example of substitute behavior is to replace inappropriate touching with shaking hands. The person learns the proper time, place, and person for intimacy. The couple rehearses "reading" each partner's cues for desires and gratification (what feels good to me). Self-control may improve with practice and positive reinforcements such as social attention and praise for success. Self-image and self-worth can be reconstructed, in part, by attention to the details of grooming and hygiene, selection and care of clothes, and attending social events for which all of these basic skills are required. Frequently the recovering person misinterprets the caring ministration of the staff as sexual attraction or "falling in love." Such misunderstandings must be diplomatically redirected as part of the training program. At the same time, the staff's respect, affection, and concern help to reinforce that the recovering person is worthy of love and attention. Meanwhile, the partner and family continue their education and training. The best prevention from alienation of partners is the continued practice of interpersonal skills in communication, expressing affection and gratification, and being together. Partner and patient can be educated, trained, and counseled individually and together by therapists who act as cocounselors. Formal sexual education can be presented individually to each partner, to the couple, or in group sessions for combined couples, for partners, or for patients. Reading and audiovisual material can serve as a supplement to the educational program. Group and peer counseling may be provided by similar methods. Groups may rehearse interpersonal and social skills, role play, and participate in recreational outings. Community training can proceed at successive stages of increasingly more difficult situations such as dining out, attending a movie, and so forth. A basic premise in all these activities is to insure the likelihood of success, and to reward that success.

The goal of all intensive hospital-based rehabilitation is to produce the knowledge, skills, and attitudes that enable the disabled person to attain full capabilities in community living and experience satisfaction and reward in life. For brain-injured persons there may be any number of intermediate steps toward that goal.

## COMMUNITY LEVELS OF CARE

Transitional living centers,[138] day hospital programs,[139] institutions for special education, vocational training centers, independent living cooperatives,[140] behavior training centers,[141] and cognitive training programs are all pathways to independence. In any of these settings, continued sexual counseling, education, and training are usually elements of the program and in many cases they are given considerable emphasis.

For the single client, opportunities for social and sexual contact can be limited or nonexistent. Family may have difficulty recognizing and dealing with this problem. Much creativity and energy is required for families to locate and organize social outlets. This intervention is often a source of conflict. Families, in their efforts to ensure social contacts, may have difficulties in defining boundaries. For example, when should the son or daughter accompany the parents to events? When are such events age-appropriate or comfortable for the child?

Peer and support groups in these institutions and in the community can be a continuing means of education, counseling, socialization, and advocacy for survivors and families.

The concerns of community reentry are illustrated by the following case study:

---

M. is a 20-year-old single female who was severely brain-injured in an automobile accident. She was in college and living in an apartment with friends prior to the injury. She had dated a variety of young men and had been "going steady" for three months prior to the accident.

M. has a supportive family. Her parents are divorced, and her father lives out of state but maintains regular contact with his daughter. There is an older brother, age 25, who is married and a younger sister, age 18, still living at home with the mother who has remarried.

M. progressed steadily through her acute hospital stay after being in deep coma for two weeks. She is paralyzed on her left side and has significant cognitive problems such as poor short-term memory, problem solving, and judgment. During the acute-care hospital stay M. acted out at times by undressing herself and hitting staff and family when frustrated. She had difficulty in expressing her wants and often could not identify her feelings other than being "mad."

The hospital staff encouraged the family to attend family education meetings at the unit. There the family was provided with information on head injury and the stages of recovery. Behavioral and cognitive problems were discussed with the social worker conducting the meeting. The team developed a behavioral plan to manage the hitting and inappropriate undressing. The speech therapist developed a basic communication board so that M. could point to such things as going to the bathroom, food, drink, sitting up, being lonely, and so forth. The psychologist assisted in developing a system to reinforce changes in behavior. When M. used the board she was praised and received extra attention. The staff began working on grooming as the patient enjoyed this activity. The family was instructed in the plan and participated actively.

Gradually the behavior problems improved. M. was able to communicate her needs verbally with more ease. She began leaving the hospital on short outings with her sister and mother.

M. was socially uninhibited and spoke to anyone around her, often repeating the same statements. The team worked with the patient on understanding the idea of strangers. The mother and sister helped M. identify who was a stranger and who was an acquaintance. M. also learned a variety of appropriate phrases to use with staff and the public to expand her conversational skills.

M. left the hospital rehabilitation program after five months. She then went home with her mother, stepfather, and sister. She began attending a day treatment program. At first she exhibited some old behaviors. She would begin undressing herself before she would enter the bathroom, then sometimes forget to close the door after entering. The team reinstituted a behavior management program cuing her on shutting the bathroom door and where and when to undress.

At home the family continued to spend most of their time with her since M.'s friends had stopped visiting her. The boyfriend visited once or twice during the early hospitalization, but then did not return.

M.'s sister requested some of her friends to accompany them to restaurants and movies. The family began attending a family support group offered by the head injury foundation. Occasionally, other family members would spend time with M. M.'s mother cut back her work hours to be available to transport M. to and from the day care program.

The day care staff alerted M.'s family to a young person's recreational head injury group. M. began attending their events. She was becoming increasingly interested in young men. She would at times get too close and touch a young man that she found attractive. M. was also found kissing and fondling another male client with whom she socialized. This was embarrassing for the sister who became angry at M. M.'s sister began counseling to not only deal with her feelings, but to develop ways to handle her sister's inappropriate behaviors. She had to learn how to explain her sister's behavior to friends and advise them how to respond to these advances.

M.'s mother discussed sexual issues with her. The mother discovered that her daughter had been sexually active prior to her injury. She had used birth control pills for contraception. M.'s mother made an appointment with the doctor and discussed birth control with M. present. It was agreed that M. should begin using birth control pills and that her mother would check to see if she remembered to take them regularly. M. had a calendar that she checked off every day when she took her pill. The doctor discussed sexually transmitted diseases and gave M. reading material. M.'s mother also enrolled her daughter in a sexual education group for people with disabilities, which was offered at the local Planned Parenthood.

M. continued to progress and eventually was able to assume a volunteer job. She traveled to and from the job by bus. M.'s mother and sister often reviewed what she should, and should not, tell strangers. They reviewed the importance of setting up a formal date where the family could meet someone she was interested in.

M. gradually continued to improve and was able to attend a community college for a couple of courses. M.'s mother made sure that her daughter had an on-campus counselor and was alerted to the group activities on campus. M. began attending a support group for survivors. Gradually her social supports grew. However, she still relied a great deal on the family for social support.

## MEDICAL-SURGICAL APPROACHES

Medical management of sexual dysfunction is directed mainly toward primary dysfunctions. Endocrine disorders are responsive to hormonal replacement. Spasticity may improve with physical measures such as heat, cooling, stretching, electrical stimulation, and other techniques that the therapist can teach the person to administer. Antispasticity drugs may be helpful. More severe and resistant forms of spasticity may require injections of drugs like phenol or alcohol into the involved muscles or peripheral nerves that control them. These procedures can reduce spasticity for periods of weeks or months, but the effects are not permanent. Certain neurosurgical or orthopedic procedures offer more permanent results. These procedures include cutting muscle tendons (tenotomies), muscle transfers,[142] cutting peripheral nerves (neurotomies), and the like. A promising recent development is the surgical placement of a dispenser of medicine in the spinal canal. This procedure allows repeated administration of the drug Baclofen into the spinal cord (intrathecal Baclofen[143]) as a control of severe spasticity.

Some movement disorders may improve with drugs. A neurological procedure called stereotactic thalamotomy (selective destruction of parts of the thalamus under x-ray guidance) has been used, albeit rarely, to treat severe and otherwise untreatable movement disorders. Some pain syndromes may be relieved by drugs, physical measures such as transcutaneous electrical stimulation (TENS: stimulation of trigger points of pain, or involved nerves through the skin), and heat. Causalgia, a type of neuritic pain often seen after injuries to the limbs, requires vigorous physical therapy, a variety of drugs, anesthetic block,[144] and, in extreme cases, surgery. The most frequently performed surgical treatment for causalgia is sympathectomy,[145] the disruption of the sympathetic nervous system.[146] (The sympathetic nervous system is a part of the autonomic nervous system[147] that controls sweating and blood vessel constriction in the involved limb.) Severe musculoskeletal deformities or contractures may require surgical correction. Some brain-injured persons develop abnormal bone formation in soft tissues (heterotopic ossification). When severe, the condition can cause pain, deformity, and joint fusion[148] in the affected area. All of these complications can adversely affect sexual activity. Treatment consists of physical therapy to prevent joint fusion, use of drugs to prevent further bone formation, occasionally joint manipulation under anesthesia, and when the abnormal bone is fully mature, surgical removal.

Impotence due to organic causes such as hormonal, neurological, or vascular[149] causes may be partial, and thus still responsive to local mechanical (vibration, rubbing, or sucking) or psychological (erotic movies or video tapes, erotic thoughts, an exciting partner, and so forth) forms of stimulation. Partial erections may be enhanced by "stuffing" the semierect penis into the vagina. Other techniques borrowed from the methods originally developed by Masters and Johnson for people with functional disorders may be of additional value. Complete organic impotence due to hormonal deficiency will likely improve with hormonal replacement therapy. When impotence is caused by reduced blood flow to the penis, blood vessel repair may be curative. With neurologic causes, impotence may respond by injecting blood vessel dilating medication into the penis (some long-term complications such as scarring of the penis may occur). The person or partner can be taught to inject the medicine before anticipated sexual activity. Another option for treating impotence is the use of a cover for the penis. Some of these external devices allow air to be sucked out from under them (Fig. 22). The vacuum effect creates penile engorgement very much like an erection. Other such devices cause engorgement by temporarily constricting the penis, thereby entrapping blood. Still others are rigid shells containing the penis. The wearer can learn to apply these devices and they are readily removed after sexual activity. Another possibility is the use of certain drugs such as yohimbine taken by

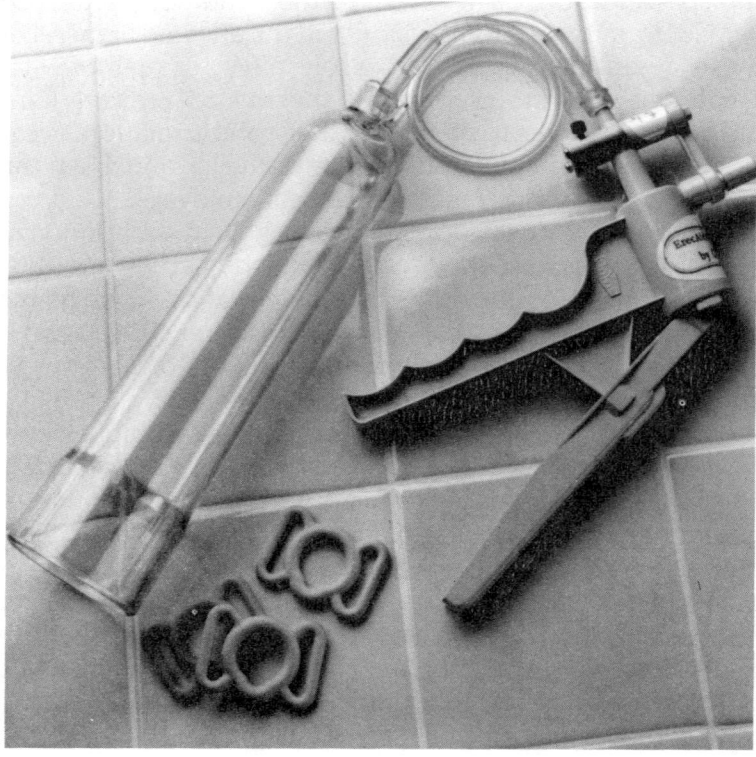

**Figure 22.** In some cases of male impotence following traumatic brain injury, this external vacuum therapy device helps achieve erection. (Courtesy of Osbon Medical Systems, Ltd.)

mouth. Some impotent persons may improve with this drug. If drugs are suspected as the cause of impotence, they can be discontinued, reduced in dosage, or replaced by other drugs. Such changes should only be undertaken under the physician's supervision. Another choice for irreversible impotence is the surgical implantation of a penile prosthesis. These devices have a number of designs, some being semirigid, or semiflexible (like a gooseneck lamp), others being inflatable for temporary erections (Fig. 23). Some impotent men and their partners prefer to choose alternatives such as oro-genital activities which do not require penile-vaginal intercourse.

Dyspareunia usually responds to specific treatment: medication for an underlying infection of the genital tract (such as vaginitis or cervicitis), local female hormone for menopausal changes of the vagina, more effective stimulation of vaginal secretions, or a vaginal lubricant.

Effective treatment of pre-existing or later-appearing medical conditions like heart, lung, kidney, and liver diseases, or anemia can restore partial or considerable sexual interest and function. Seizures are generally well controlled by anticonvulsant drugs. Often these drugs produce the undesirable side effects of drowsiness, reduced mental efficiency, and poor coordination in susceptible brain-injured persons. A notable exception is the drug carbamazapine (Tegretol), which rarely exhibits these side effects, although occasionally it can produce others.

Sexual disabilities related to mental dysfunctions may require both medical and psychological management. Anti-depressant drugs such as amitriptyline have been helpful in managing depressive states and in reducing agitated behavior. Other agents, many relating to the stimulation or suppression of neurotransmitters, have been used to treat agitation. Anti-parkinson drugs such as L-Dopa and central nervous system stimulating drugs have been used to treat problems of lethargy, slowness, and lack of initiative. As with any drugs, these medicines are prescribed by physicians who

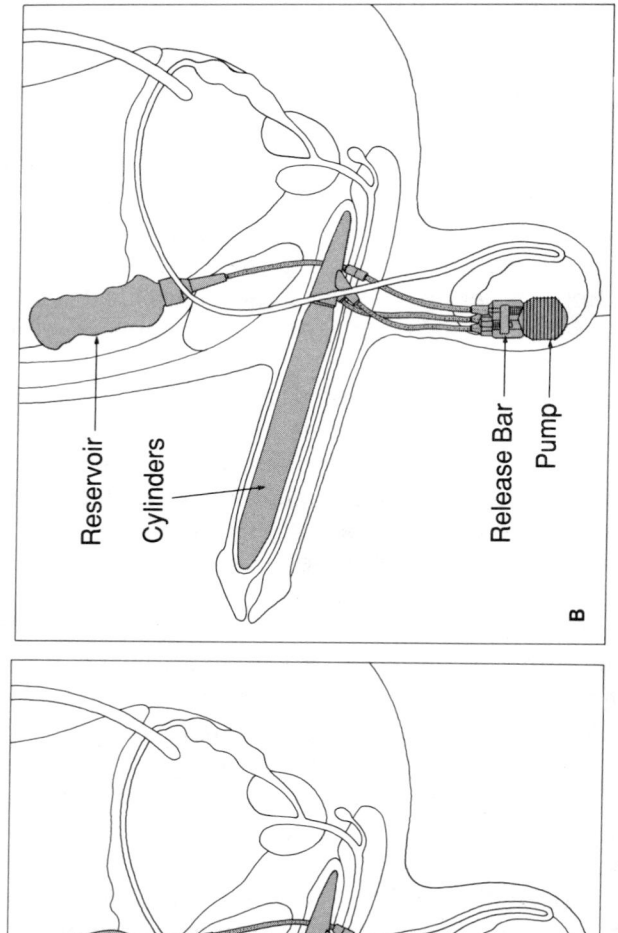

**Figure 23.** Some cases of irreversible impotence can be treated with the surgical implantation of a penile prosthesis. (Courtesy of Mentor Corporation, Santa Barbara, California.)

carefully consider their possible side effects and interactions with other medications.

Deformities of the head, face, and neck, and other cosmetic defects can be improved or corrected by plastic surgery. Excessive salivation or drooling may respond to drugs or certain types of oral surgery. Contraceptive techniques including birth control pills, condoms, diaphragms, tubal ligation, vasectomy, and so forth should be available for routine purposes or for the protection of vulnerable uninhibited females. Condoms have the additional protective function of preventing the transmission of AIDS and other sexually transmitted diseases. Sexually violent males have been treated with female hormones or male-hormone-inhibiting drugs.

Rehabilitation of alcohol and other drug abuse entails specific programs supported by medications such as tranquilizers, vitamin supplements, sulfarim (Antabuse), and substitution of methadone for heroin or related narcotics.

The medical and surgical approaches to treatment should be closely integrated with a total plan of management. More often than not, sexual problems are multiple and causes are both physical and psychosocial. Furthermore, some of these problems are not suddenly solved or cured. Thus treatment may be required over a period of time, and improvement occurs gradually. Therefore, treatment programs must address the full array of dysfunctions and consider each component of treatment as it affects the whole for both the patient and the partner. Table 13 provides a summary of the forms of treatment approaches for each type of sexual dysfunction.

## SPECIAL CONSIDERATIONS IN MANAGEMENT

### Homosexuality

About 10 percent of us are predominantly homosexual (gay[150] or lesbian[151]). Often homosexuality is not recognized by the

**Table 13**

## SUMMARY OF TREATMENT APPROACHES

| Types of Sexual Dysfunction | Treatment |
|---|---|
| Sex drive and interest | Hormone replacement |
| | Neurotransmitters and related drugs* |
| | Discontinuation or modification of responsible medicines |
| | Drug rehabilitation |
| | Reconditioning and correcting nutritional problems |
| | Pain control |
| | Control of medical problems |
| | Psychological and medical treatment of emotional causes (depression, anxiety, and so forth) |
| Sexual responses | Medical-surgical and/or psychological treatment of impotence |
| | Discontinuation or modification of responsible medicines |
| | Drug rehabilitation |
| | Psychological and medical treatment of emotional causes |
| | Hormone replacement |
| | Medical-surgical treatment of neurological blood vessel disorders |
| | Medical treatment of gynecological conditions |
| | Vaginal lubrication |
| | Adequate stimulation |
| Fertility | Hormone replacement |
| | Medical-surgical treatment of nonendocrine causes of infertility |
| | Artificial insemination, donor sperm or ovum, donor implantation into uterus |

**Table 13**

**SUMMARY OF TREATMENT APPROACHES** (*Continued*)

| *Types of Sexual Dysfunction* | *Treatment* |
|---|---|
| Mobility | Medical-surgical and therapy treatment of spasticity, movement disorders, deformities, poor motor control, and poor balance |
| | Therapy training of mobility skills and assistance skills of partner |
| | Reconditioning, strengthening |
| | Environmental modifications and equipment |
| Self-care skills | Same as mobility |
| | Therapy training of skills and partner assistance |
| | Cognitive retraining |
| | Adaptive devices |
| Sensation | Sensory retraining |
| | Perceptual retraining |
| | Pain management |
| | Prevention of injury training |
| Communications and oral functions | Speech-language therapy |
| | Alternate systems of communication |
| | Cognitive retraining |
| | Therapy training of oral motor skills |
| Cosmesis | Surgical correction of defects |
| | Reconditioning, strengthening |
| | Correction of nutritional problems |
| | Hormone replacement |
| | Medical treatment of skin eruptions |
| | Psychological treatment |
| Mental | Cognitive retraining |
| | Behavior training                    (*continued*) |

**Table 13**

## SUMMARY OF TREATMENT APPROACHES (*Continued*)

| Types of Sexual Dysfunction | Treatment |
| --- | --- |
| | Perceptual retraining |
| | Special education |
| | Psychiatric and psychological counseling and therapy for patient, partner, and family |
| | Medications for depression, behavioral disorders, thought disorders, to improve alertness, and so forth |
| Social | Psychological and social work counseling and therapy for patient, partner, and family |
| | Educational programs for patient, partner, family, and community |
| | Marital counseling |
| | Sex counseling and therapy |
| | Training of social and interpersonal skills |
| | Vocational rehabilitation |
| | Peer and advocacy support groups for patient and family |
| | Drug and alcohol rehabilitation |
| | Avocational, leisure skills training |

*Still experimental

health care team. The notion that all brain-injured patients prefer the opposite sex (are heterosexual) can lead to inappropriate sexual rehabilitation goals and management, patient feelings of embarrassment or guilt, and failure to involve a significant partner in the program. The team can become embroiled in conflicts between families, patients, and partners, with efforts to "protect" the patient on both sides. The situation may become bitter, requiring extreme discretion and avoidance of moralizing by the team. The homosexual partner should be given the same consideration and access as a heterosexual companion to educational, training, and counseling services.

Institutional, community, and national resources for gays and lesbians can be made available to homosexual couples in order to facilitate the rehabilitation program and community reentry.

## Pregnancy, Childbirth, and Child Care

Women of childbearing age are generally tested for pregnancy at the time of their brain injury. Fetal death can occur as the result of maternal death or maternal abdominal-pelvic injury involving the uterus. Discovery of pregnancy alters some of the emergency care of the woman. The uterus is shielded from x-ray. Drugs causing birth defects or severe side effects to the fetus are avoided. Techniques of anesthesia and artificial ventilation are modified. Seizure control is monitored closely, and late in pregnancy, the back-lying (supine) position is avoided. Labor requires close vigilance of seizure control as well. Some medicines, including certain antiseizure drugs, can cause side effects in the breast-fed infant.

Mildly, moderately, or even severely disabled mothers may, with training and the help of family and community resources, continue to care for their children. Severely cognitively disabled mothers need assistance in child care. If family and community support services are inadequate, temporary or permanent placement of the child may be required. State laws vary on this matter. Legal counsel should be obtained before a decision is made.

## Contraception

Contraception[152] is another critical area requiring detailed education and training for the injured person, partner, and often the family. The methods of contraception are either reversible or irreversible. In the first category, condoms (for males or females), diaphragms, and spermicidal chemicals, intrauterine devices[153] (IUDs), cervical caps,[154] oral cyclic female hormones (the pill), and most recently, long-acting injectable or implantable hormones are considerations. There are advantages and disadvantages to each of these methods. Poor patient compliance due to memory and other mental deficits may require that condom usage, diaphragm placement, or oral hormone administration be supervised or performed by the partner. There are some risks with the intrauterine device such as pelvic infection. Oral hormonal contraception can increase the risk of blood vessel clotting.

Permanent contraception can be electively performed by either of two surgical procedures: for women, tubal ligation (severing and tying the two fallopian tubes through a small abdominal incision); for men, vasectomy (severing and tying the vas deferens in the male scrotum through a small incision on each side). In the case of severe mental deficits, legal guardianship and psychiatric or psychological consultation may be required before surgery is performed.

The choices of contraceptive method are best made after consultation with a physician who is both knowledgeable concerning contraception and well-informed about the individual's circumstances.

## Sexually Transmitted Diseases

Because of their uninhibited behaviors, poor judgment, and indifference to the consequences of indiscriminate sexual activity, some brain-injured persons are susceptible to sexually transmitted diseases (venereal diseases). AIDS is the most devastating of these infectious disorders. Thus far, there is no specific agent that will eradicate the virus causing this disease. However, AIDS is preventable. Table 14 lists the major steps in the prevention of AIDS.

Other venereal diseases include gonorrhea, syphilis, chlamydial infections,[155] herpes of the genital organs,[156] venereal warts,[157] and trichomonas infections.[158] There are several other rare forms of infections. Patients and their families can be educated about these infections, particularly as to how they are prevented. Routine use of condoms can largely avert them. With the exception of herpes, all can be cured by early recognition and treatment. Herpes is now controllable with the prescription drug acyclovir.

The following case report demonstrates some of the

### Table 14

### PREVENTIVE MEASURES AGAINST AIDS

Avoidance of multiple sexual partners

Use of sterile needles, syringes, and other materials by IV drug users

Use of condoms for sexual activities

Avoidance of direct contact with vaginal secretions, semen, and blood (use of gloves by health care personnel and others who must handle these items)

Screening of blood donors for AIDS

Testing of blood and blood products for the AIDS virus before medical use (blood transfusions, blood products for hemophiliacs, and so forth)

Identification of AIDS virus carriers among susceptible populations (homosexuals, IV drug users, prostitutes, and persons exposed to AIDS victims)

Avoidance of "deep kissing"*

*There is no proof that tears or saliva transmit AIDS.

special problems we have described and offers treatment approaches that the family can initiate.

---

A 16-year-old girl has been home with her parents for several months after being discharged from the hospital. Five months ago, she sustained a closed head injury in an automobile collision. She was judged to have moderate brain damage (Glasgow Coma Score on hospital admission was nine). The girl has a very mild left hemiparesis, but retains moderately severe deficits in mental and social functions. She is childish, openly seductive, and uninhibited about sexual thoughts and activities. One day she casually reveals to her mother that she befriended a small group of construction workers while she was walking about the neighborhood. On several occasions, she has agreed to accompany them on drives to a secluded spot where she has engaged with each of them in sexual acts. She seems unconcerned about the matter and of its possible consequences. Her mother is understandably frantic. What should this mother do now?

As difficult as it seems, the mother should control the urge to panic. She should express her concern about this revelation, and state the reasons why. However, the mother should thank her daughter for sharing a confidential matter with her. She should then propose several immediate steps to her daughter: (1) to inform her father and seek his ideas, (2) to schedule the daughter to see a physician to be sure that she is not pregnant, that she does not have a sexually transmitted disease, and that a method of contraception is established, (3) to temporarily suspend the daughter's unsupervised activities in order to stop the uninhibited sexual activities. These immediate steps should be explained in straightforward terms without anger or moralizing. As soon as the father is fully informed, he can assist his wife and daughter in further planning. The parents should meet preliminarily to further discuss the immediate and later planning and resolve any differences between them. The family should seek legal advice about the options in the event that the daughter is pregnant. They may need counseling on the ethical aspects of abortion as well. They can seek a lawyer's recommendations about notifying the supervisor of the men involved about the events and their daughter's circumstances. (Should the men be prosecuted?) To insure that the daughter will avoid further temptation, the parents can devise a behavior plan. The daughter will be supervised at all times by a responsible person until she has demonstrated control of her behavior. The principles of eliminating the undesired behavior, encouraging substitute desired behaviors, allowing opportunity for and endorsing masturbation in a private setting, creating a system of reward to strengthen desirable behaviors, and teaching and rehearsing those behaviors have already been detailed in the earlier case of the boy who exhibited and masturbated in public.

Parental education and training for the daughter can supplement sexual counseling by a qualified professional. The girl should be provided with basic information about contraception and prevention of sexually transmitted disease. Opportunities for alternative behaviors can be provided by chaperoned social activities with peers who understand the nature of the girl's disability and are rehearsed in how to behave with her. Parents can instruct and rehearse their daughter in conducting herself in socially appropriate ways. They can help reinforce the idea that the path to restored respect, self-image, and self-worth is through mastery of these behaviors.

## LONG-TERM FOLLOW-UP CARE

The survivor and family continue to make adjustments to the consequences of brain injury for long periods of time; often their lifetime. Families may not fully realize the implications of the injury until considerable time has passed. Earlier over-riding concerns about survival and medical and physical issues shift to the persisting or increasing social, behavioral, and emotional problems. These later problems become more apparent as the survivor reengages in community life and work. Too often, social supports fade as friends and other family members distance themselves from these unyielding burdens. The resulting isolation can provoke yet greater stresses on the remaining family and survivor. Anger and/or depression follow for all concerned. Individual, marital, or family counseling is usually indicated. Support groups can help diminish feelings of isolation, loneliness, and low self-esteem, and increase understanding of the problems at hand.

As with other aspects of rehabilitation, sexual assessment and management should continue after return to the community. At the critical point of community reentry, issues often become more acute. The emphasis of treatment may shift mainly to psychosocial and communication skills. Early after discharge, frequent revisions in the training programs are the general rule. Changes of sexual function with the passage of time, aging, during critical stresses and changes of family and marital interrelationships may be expected. Cues for help by patient or family should constantly be searched for. These cues may be direct, in the form of frank observations, questions, or actions. For example, they could be expressions concerning parenting, attractiveness, relationships, or aggressive sexual behavior. However, they may be subtle, a seemingly casual remark or gesture. The treatment team, partner, family, and sometimes the survivor can learn to be sensitive to these cues. Just as the restoration and maintenance of life functions is a lifelong process, so is sexual function. The partner and family must assist the health care team in periodically reviewing sexual function in anticipation of possible changes and in striving to preserve open, candid lines of communication on a subject that deserves the same attention as our blood pressure, heart, or any other health issue.

Our concluding thought is that a satisfying sexual life can be a basis for other life fulfillments. Freud asserted that love and work are the most gratifying aspects of living. We see tangible evidence of that belief in our professional experience. The sense of self-worth that comes from a fully expressed loving relationship usually translates into productive, rewarding endeavors at home, at work, and in the community.

# Where Can You Get Help?

What if you have not had access to the types of services that we have described even though your partner or relative has completed an intensive rehabilitation program? What if you need additional advice or services that you cannot obtain from the original site of acute care?

An understanding primary care physician may be an immediate resource. That physician can refer you to other community resources as well as provide service. A local or regional chapter of the National Head Injury Foundation can be a starting point in obtaining help. Larger communities usually have rehabilitation counselors or social workers who can offer the following information on available resources: their cost, whether health insurance provides for the service in question, the details of application, and so forth. A local or regional rehabilitation center with a designated brain injury program can be a source of extensive information as well as specific services. Specialty clinics in sexuality and impotence are often hospital-based, and like most health services, including information and referral services, are listed in the yellow pages of telephone directories. Certified sex counselors are available in sexuality clinics. All states have a vocational rehabilitation agency with a central office 5700 Old Orchard Road Skokie, Illinois 60077 (708) 966-0095 in the state capital as well as regional offices.

National resources to be considered include:

**The National Head Injury Foundation, Inc.**
1140 Connecticut Ave. N.W.
Suite 812
Washington, D.C. 20036
(202) 296-6443

## ADDITIONAL RESOURCES

**The Task Force on Sexuality and Disability of the American Congress of Rehabilitation Medicine**
5700 Old Orchard Road
Skokie, IL 60077
(708) 966-0095

**Interdisciplinary Special Interest Group on Head Injury of the American Congress of Rehabilitation Medicine**
5700 Old Orchard Road
Skokie, IL 60077
(708) 966-0095

**Sex Information and Education Council of the United States**
84 Fifth Avenue, Suite 407
New York, NY 10011

**Sexuality and Disability Training Center**
University of Michigan Medical Center
Department of Physical Medicine and Rehabilitation
1500 E. Medical Center Drive
Ann Arbor, MI 48109
(313) 936-7067

**Sexuality and Disability Training Center**
Boston University Medical Center
88 E. Newton Street
Boston, MA 02118
(617) 638-7358

American Association of Sex Education Counselors and
Therapists
435 N. Michigan Avenue, Suite 1717
Chicago, IL 60611
(312) 644-0828

National Organization on Disability
2100 Pennsylvania Avenue, N.W.
Washington, D.C. 20037
(202) 293-5960

The Head Injury Association of Canada
P.O. Box 5283—Station F
Ottawa, Ontario, Canada
K2C 3H5
(613) 723-7798

AIDS National Hotline
1-800-342-AIDS
1-800-HIV-INFO

Planned Parenthood Federation
810 7th Ave., 11th Floor
New York, NY 10019
(212) 541-7800

Gay & Lesbian Task Force
1734 14th St. N.W.
Washington, D.C. 20009
(202) 332-6483

## CHILDREN'S RESOURCES

National Information Center for Children and Youth with
Handicaps
P.O. Box 1492
Washington, D.C. 20013
1-800-999-5599

**National Center for Youth with Disabilities**
Adolescent Health Program
University of Minnesota
P.O. Box 721-UMHC
Harvard St. at East River Road
Minneapolis, MN 55455
1-800-333-NCYD or
(612) 626-2825

**National Rehabilitation Information Center**
8455 Colesville Rd., Suite 935
Silver Spring, MD 20910-3319
1-800-346-2742

**Council for Exceptional Children**
1920 Association Drive
Reston, VA 22091-1589
(703) 620-3660

**Federation for Children with Special Needs**
95 Berkeley St., Suite 104
Boston, MA 02116
(617) 482-2915

# References
# and Reading List

## DEVELOPMENTAL PARENTING

Adams, T. *Living From the Inside Out* 1987. Write: Teresa Adams, 1331 Philip St., New Orleans, LA 70130

Bradshaw, J. *The Family*, Deerfield Beach, FL: Health Communications, 1988

Drinkmeyer, D. and McKay, G. *Systemic Training for Effective Parenting* (STEP); *The Parent's Handbook*, 3rd Edition, 1989. Write: American Guidance Service, P.O. Box 99, Publisher's Building, Circle Pines, MN 55014-1796; 1-800-328-2560

Efron, D. and Rowe, B. *The Strategic Parenting Manual*, 1987. Write: J.S.S.T. Box 2484 STN A, London, Ontario, Canada N6A 467

Ginott, H. *Between Parent & Child*, New York: Avon Books, 1969

Gordon, T. *Parent Effectiveness Training*, New York: New American Library, 1970

Mason, D., Jensen, G., and Ryzewicz, C. *No More Tantrums . . . and Other Good News*, Chicago: Contemporary Books, 1987

## AIDS RESOURCES FOR PARENTS

AIDS *Prevention Guide for Parents*. Free booklet for parents of teenagers. National Centers for Disease Control, 1-800-458-5231

Hausherr, R: *Children and the AIDS Virus*. Clarion Books, 52 Vanderbilt Ave., New York, NY 10017, $13.95

Quackenbush, M. and Villareal, S: *Does AIDS Hurt?* Educating Young Children about AIDS, 5–10 Network Publications, P.O. Box 1830, Santa Cruz, CA 95061-1830, $14.95

## HEAD INJURY PARENTING INFORMATION

Lash, M. *When Your Child is Seriously Injured in an Accident . . . The Emotional Impact on Families*. Research and Training Center in Rehabilitation and Childhood Trauma, Attention: M. Lash, Rehabilitation Medicine, 750 Washington St., # 75K-R, Boston, MA 02111; (617) 956-5036 or (617) 956-5032, free

Pieper, B. *Sisters and Brothers, Brothers and Sisters in the Family Affected by Traumatic Brain Injury*. New York State Head Injury Association, 855 Central Ave., Albany, New York 12206; (518) 459-7911 or 1-800-228-8201

Pieper, B. *In Home Family Supports: What Families of Youngsters with Traumatic Brain Injury Really Need*. New York State Head Injury Association, 855 Central Ave., Albany, New York 12206; (518) 459-7911 or 1-800-228-8201

Pieper, B. *Traumatic Brain Injury: What the Teacher Needs to Know*. New York State Head Injury Association, 855 Central Ave., Albany, New York 12206; (518) 459-7911 or 1-800-228-8201

## ADULT HEAD INJURY

Barbach, L. *For Yourself: The Fulfillment of Female Sexuality*. New York: Doubleday, 1975

Benda, S., (ed.). *Head Injury Education Manual for Patients and Families*, 1987. Department of Outreach Services, Good Samaritan Medical Center, P.O. Box 2989, 1111 E. McDowell Road, Phoenix, AZ 85062

Berroll, S. *Issues of Sexuality in Head Injured Adults*. National Head Injury Foundation, $1.00

Blackerby, W. *Disruption of Sexuality Can Have Traumatic Effect*. National Head Injury Foundation, $1.00

Blackerby, E.F. and Porter, S. *Psychosocial Aspects of Sexual Dysfunction in Head Injury*. In Horn, L.J. and Cope, D.N. (eds.), *Traumatic Brain Injury, State of the Art Reviews*. Philadelphia: Hanley and Belfus, 1989, pp. 143–155

Blackerby, W.F. (ed.). *Sexuality and Head Injury*. Journal of Head Trauma Rehabilitation 5(2) 1990.

Broller, F. and Frank, E. *Sexual Dysfunction in Neurological Disorders: Diagnosis, Management and Rehabilitation*. New York: Raven Press, 1982

Griffith, E.R., Cole, S, and Cole, T. *Sexuality and Sexual Dysfunction*. In Rosenthan, M. et al. (eds.), *Rehabilitation of the Adult and Child with Traumatic Brain Injury*, 2nd Edition, Philadelphia: FA Davis, 1990

*Impotence*. Urologic Clinics of North America. 15.1, 1988.

*Information on AIDS for the Practicing Physician*, Volume 3: Recommendations to Family, Friends and Household Contacts, p. 18, and Guidelines for the General Public, p. 19, July 1987. American Medical Association, 535 N. Dearborn St., Chicago, IL 60610

Kolodny, R.C., Masters, W.H., and Johnson V.E. *Textbook of Sexual Medicine*. Boston: Little, Brown, 1979

Kruetzer, J.S. and Zasler, N.D. *Psychosexual Consequences of Traumatic Brain Injury: Methodology and Preliminary Findings.* Brain Injury 3:177–186, 1989

Lezak, M.D. *Living with the Characterologically Altered Brain Injured Patient.* J Clin Psychiatry 39:592–598, 1978

Masters, W. and Johnson, V. *Human Sexual Response.* Boston: Little, Brown, 1966

Plum, F. and Posner, J. *Neurologic Disease.* In Andreoli, T, Carpenter, C, Plum, F, and Smith, L (eds.), *Cecil Essentials of Medicine.* Philadelphia: WB Saunders, 1986, p. 762

Price, J.R. *Sexuality Following Traumatic Brain Injury.* In Miner, M.E. and Wagner, K.A. (eds.), *Neurotrauma.* Butterworths-Heinemann, 1988, pp. 173–180

Restak, R. *The Brain,* New York: Bantam Books, 1984

*Sexuality and Disability: A Bibliography.* National Head Injury Foundation, $1.00

Ylvisaker, M. and Gobble, E.M. *Community Re-Entry for Head Injured Adults.* Austin, TX: College Hill Press, 1987

Zasler, N. *Sexuality Issues After Traumatic Brain Injury; Sexuality Update.* National Task Force on Sexuality and Disability, Volume I, Number 1, September, 1988

Zilbergeld, B. *Male Sexuality.* New York: Bantam Books, 1978

# Glossary

**TERMS DEFINED IN ORDER OF APPEARANCE**

1. *traumatic brain injury:* damage to the brain and/or brainstem due to mechanical injury. Most frequent causes are vehicular accidents. Other causes are falls, violence (missile wounds, stabbings, blows to the head), and sports injuries.

2. *ejaculation:* expulsion of seminal fluid from the penis, usually associated with the experience of orgasm.

3. *dysfunction:* a decreased functional capacity resulting from a physical or mental impairment. Synonymous with disability.

4. *seminal fluid:* the liquid containing the male sex cells (spermatozoa) that is expelled from the penis during climax. Also called semen.

5. *orgasm:* the paroxysm of physical and emotional excitement occurring at the height of sexual excitement. Also called climax. In the male, normally accompanied by ejaculation.

6. *nocturnal emissions:* expelling of semen from the penis at night, usually associated with sexual dreams: "wet dreams."

7. *genitalia:* the male and female organs of reproduction. Also called genital organs or genitals.

8. *labia minora:* (the smaller lips) sensitive tissue surrounding the vaginal opening, rich in blood vessels

and therefore readily engorged and opened with sexual excitement.

9. **clitoris:** a small erectile body of the female genitalia. Equivalent to the penis.

10. **ovaries:** the paired female pelvic genital organs producing the egg (ovum). Also the organs producing female hormones.

11. **fallopian tubes:** the two tubes connected to the uterus, carrying the egg (ovum) from the ovary to the uterus. Normally the site of fertilization of the egg.

12. **uterus:** the female pelvic organ where the fertilized egg implants, develops, and grows into a baby. Its inner lining sheds each month from puberty to menopause as a menstrual period. Also called the womb.

13. **testicle:** the paired male genital organ which is equivalent to the female ovary. Also called testes (plural). Site of production of the male sperm cells (spermatozoa) and of most male hormones.

14. **epididymis:** paired oblong bodies attached to the testicles. Site of storage of mature sperm cells.

15. **vas deferens:** the two tubes which carry sperm from the testicles to the penis. By cutting and tying the tubes, a man can be made sterile, although the testicle continues to make male hormones.

16. **spermatozoa:** the mature sex cell made in the testicle. Also called sperm.

17. **seminal vesicles:** paired bodies adjacent to the prostate gland which contribute secretions to the seminal fluid.

18. **prostate gland:** a gland surrounding the neck of the bladder and first part of the urethra in the male. It contributes secretions to the seminal fluid.

19. **brain:** the general term describing the highest centers of the central nervous system: the brainstem, the

diencephalon, and the cerebrum. Often the term is used to indicate the cerebrum proper.

20. *cerebrum*:   the highest center and largest part of the brain, consisting of two halves called cerebral hemispheres. Each hemisphere is divided into four lobes: frontal, temporal, parietal, and occipital.

21. *corpus callosum*:   the large body of white matter through which nerve fibers cross from one cerebral hemisphere to the other. Extensive damage to the corpus callosum can cause "disconnection" of right and left brains and produce unusual syndromes.

22. *frontal lobe*:   the part of the brain (cerebrum) located in front of the parietal lobe and separated from it by a fissure.

23. *prefrontal area*:   that part of the cerebrum lying in the very front of the brain; often damaged in brain injury.

24. *parietal lobe*:   the part of the brain (cerebrum) located behind the frontal lobe, above the temporal lobe, and in front of the occipital lobe.

25. *temporal lobe*:   the part of the brain (cerebrum) located below the parietal lobe and separated from it by a fissure.

26. *limbic system*:   a group of deep cortical structures connecting to the hypothalamus; governs memory, emotions, and basic drives, including the sex drive.

27. *occipital lobe*:   the part of the brain located behind the parietal and temporal lobes.

28. *gray matter*:   the portion of brain, brainstem, and cord that is composed predominantly of cell bodies.

29. *cerebral cortex*:   the outer layer of the cerebral hemispheres, consisting of gray matter.

30. *white matter*:   the portion of brain, brainstem, and cord that is composed predominantly of nerve fibers.

31. *lateral ventricles*:   the two largest cavities of the brain,

deep within each hemisphere, filled with cerebral fluid and connecting to two other smaller ventricles; part of the internal circulation system carrying cerebrospinal fluid.

32. **cerebrospinal fluid:** the clear watery liquid made and circulated in the ventricular system of the brain and throughout the space between layers of the meninges of brain and spinal cord. The fluid pressure is a measure of the severity of head injury.

33. **intracranial pressure:** the pressure within the brain, as measured by the pressure of the cerebrospinal fluid; measured, in cases of severe brain injury, as a surgical procedure by which a valve or catheter is placed within the skull.

34. **diencephalon:** the interbrain, deep in the cerebrum, consisting of the thalamus and adjacent related nerve centers; located just above the brainstem.

35. **basal ganglia:** paired groups of cell bodies located deep in the cerebral hemispheres. They regulate the initiation of movement and posture. Damage to these structures causes movement disorders such as parkinsonism.

36. **hypothalamus:** a nerve center which controls the pituitary gland, the autonomic nervous system, food intake, sexual rhythms, and emotions; located just beneath the thalamus in the diencephalon.

37. **pituitary gland:** the small gland located in a bony cup at the base of the skull and attached to the brain beneath the hypothalamus. Governs the activity of ovaries, testicles, thyroid, and adrenal gland. Also regulates body water.

38. **thalamus:** the major relay station for sensory pathways ascending to the sensory strip of the cortex; located in the diencephalon, just above the brainstem.

**39. brainstem:**   that part of the central nervous system between the spinal cord and the diencephalon. It is located within the skull beneath the cerebral hemispheres. In order, it consists of the midbrain, the pons, and the medulla. The brainstem is attached to the cerebellum.

**40. midbrain (mesencephalon):**   the first part of the brainstem, between the diencephalon and the pons.

**41. pons:**   the part of the brainstem between the midbrain (mesencephalon) and the medulla.

**42. medulla:**   the last part of the brainstem, between the pons and the spinal cord.

**43. cerebellum:**   the part of the brainstem that governs coordination and balance.

**44. cranial nerves:**   12 pairs of nerves coming from the brain (the optic and olfactory) and the brainstem that provide the sensations of vision, hearing, balance, taste, and smell, as well as muscle functions to the head area and autonomic nervous system.

**45. reticular activating system:**   an extensive network of nerve cells within the brainstem which controls alertness, attention, vigilance, and sleep.

**46. spinal cord:**   the extension of the central nervous system from the brainstem lodged within the spinal column (the spine). Contains long pathways to and from the brain and is the site of origin of the spinal nerves going to and from the trunk, body organs, and limb.

**47. diffuse injury:**   a widespread or generalized injury to a tissue or organ such as the brain.

**48. anoxia:**   absence of oxygen supply to tissue.

**49. CT scan:**   (or CAT scan), computerized tomography of the brain; an x-ray study of the brain consisting of multiple serial cross sections (axial views) from top to bottom. An important diagnostic study to detect bleeding, hydrocephalus, and other early or late complications of brain injury as well as the extent and location of injury.

50. *neurotransmitters*:  chemicals made in the nervous system that serve as messengers throughout the nervous system aiding or interfering with the functions of nerve cells.

51. *coup injury*:  an injury to the brain directly beneath the site of a blow to the head.

52. *contrecoup injury*:  an injury to the brain opposite the site of a blow to the head as a result of a shift of the brain causing the opposite side to strike against the inner wall of the skull.

53. *open head injury*:  an injury where there is a penetration of the scalp and skull through to brain tissue.

54. *closed head injury*:  a brain injury where there is no penetration from the scalp and skull through to the brain tissue. Often there is no injury of scalp or skull with diffuse brain injuries associated with vehicular accidents.

55. *nuclear magnetic resonance imaging* (NMRI):  or magnetic resonance imaging (MRI), a diagnostic tool for detailed study of the brain that uses electrical signals from the brain in response to applied radio frequency signals; it displays finer details of tissue and better access to brainstem than CT scan. The latter is less expensive, gives better detail of bone, and is still the ''gold standard'' radiological study after brain injury.

56. *Glasgow Coma Scale*:  a numerical score given to head-injured patients at regular intervals starting immediately after injury. A score of 7 or less routinely indicates that the person is in coma. A maximum score of 15 indicates that the person can speak coherently, obeys commands to move, and can spontaneously open his eyes. The scoring system allows early cate-

gorizing of patients as having severe, moderate, or mild injuries.

57. *posttraumatic amnesia* **(PTA):**    memory loss of events that occur after brain injury. The length of time of PTA is closely correlated to the severity of brain injury and the duration of coma.

58. *aphasia:*    one of several types of inability to understand, process, or produce speech. Related to disease or injury of the cortex or subcortex of the brain.

59. *dysgraphia:*    difficulty in writing.

60. *agraphia:*    inability to write. Related to a disorder of the brain.

61. *alexia:*    inability to read. Related to a disorder of the brain.

62. *hemiparesis:*    weakness of one side of the body caused by brain, brainstem, or spinal cord disorders.

63. *hemiplegia:*    paralysis of one side of the body caused by brain, brainstem, or spinal cord disorders.

64. *hemisensory deficit:*    alteration or loss of sensation of one side of the body caused by brain, brainstem, or spinal cord disorders.

65. *spasticity:*    exaggerated reflexes, especially in the form of muscle spasms causing abnormal postures and movements. Caused by injuries to the parts of the brain, brainstem, or spinal cord that are concerned with motor control.

66. *apraxia:*    inability or difficulty in responding to a request for a specific skilled movement when there is no paralysis or inability to understand the request. The movement can be achieved spontaneously. Seen with certain brain disorders.

67. *hemianopsia:*    loss of vision involving half of the entire field of vision; caused by damage to optic tract of one cerebral hemisphere.

**68. *impotence*:** inability of a male to achieve or maintain an erection. Condition may have always been present, or may occur after earlier period of potency. Causes can be physical, psychological, or both.

**69. *aprosodia*:** inability to produce musicality, inflection, or rhythm of speech, thus giving no emotional tone or nuance to speech; seen with nondominant hemisphere injuries.

**70. *perception*:** the interpretation of all types of sensory information: visual, taste, smell, hearing, touch, pain, position sense, and so forth. The correlation of these sensory inputs with past and present experiences.

**71. *autotopagnosia*:** the inability to recognize one's own body parts, due to damage of the nondominant parietal lobe. A type of perceptual problem.

**72. *anosagnosia*:** inability of a person to realize he has a medical disorder or disability; a perceptual defect due to nondominant parietal lobe injuries.

**73. *astereognosis*:** inability to perceive the texture, shape, and other qualities by which to identify objects by touch when the basic sensation of touch is present.

**74. *cognitive*:** relating to metal functions of memory, awareness, attention, concentration, reasoning, understanding, perception, and so forth.

**75. *disinhibition*:** difficulty in controlling urges and impulses to speak, act, or emote.

**76. *abulia*:** absence of motivation; inability or deficiency in initiating movement, behavior, or thought; seen with prefrontal area brain injuries.

**77. *perseveration*:** repeatedly saying, doing, or thinking the same thing; seen often with damage to the cerebral cortex.

**78. *endocrine glands*:** glands which secrete chemicals called hormones into the blood stream. The hormones regulate the functions of body organs.

79. **septum:** a double walled structure located immediately below the corpus callosum; part of the limbic system. Injuries to the septal area have produced impotence.

80. **exhibitionism:** open display of one's body or body parts for the purpose of attracting sexual interest.

81. **transvestism:** the practice of dressing in clothes of the opposite sex.

82. **fetishism:** the practice of loving or obtaining sexual gratification from an inanimate object; the object represents the symbol of a loved person.

83. **amenorrhea:** absence of menstrual period(s).

84. **polycystic ovaries:** ovaries containing multiple cysts; associated with endocrine disorders.

85. **Kluver-Bucy syndrome:** excessive sexual expression, psychic blindness, docility, and indiscriminate placing of objects in mouth. Seen with two-sided injuries of part of temporal lobes.

86. **visual field cut:** loss of vision confined to one part of the entire field of vision.

87. **cortical blindness:** loss of vision (usually incomplete) due to a disorder of occipital lobe(s).

88. **parkinsonian syndrome:** a disorder involving the basal ganglia that is characterized by tremor, rigidity, and slow movement. Also called parkinsonism. It has various causes including injury and stroke. Parkinson disease is one type of syndrome. Its cause is uncertain.

89. **rigidity:** a disorder of muscle tone caused by basal ganglia or brainstem disorders. It produces abnormal postures and resistance to movement of limbs.

90. **ballism:** involuntary movement disorder characterized by flinging, throwing motions of the limbs; due to disorders of the basal ganglia.

91. **athetosis:**   involuntary movement disorder character-ized by wormlike writhing motions; due to disorders of the basal ganglia.

92. **chorea:**   involuntary movement disorder character-ized by irregular jerking motions of body or limbs; due to basal ganglion disorders.

93. **dystonia:**   involuntary movement disorder character-ized by sustained, often bizarre posturing of body or limbs; due to basal ganglion disorders.

94. **thalamic pain:**   a severe form of pain, usually involving half of the body and accompanied by distressing emo-tional feelings; caused by damage to the thalamus.

95. **precocious puberty:**   pre-adolescent development of the primary sex organs and secondary sexual charac-teristics such as breast development in girls and growth of facial hair and lowering of voice in boys.

96. **diabetes insipidus:**   excessive urination due to the inability of the kidneys to reabsorb water. The kidney is regulated by a hormone secreted by the posterior pituitary gland. Damage to that part of the pituitary results in deficiency or absence of the hormone (anti-diuretic hormone), and produces this syndrome.

97. **prolactin:**   a hormone secreted by the anterior pitu-itary gland; responsible for breast production of milk in the normal postpartum female.

98. **libido:**   sex drive or interest.

99. **ataxia:**   uncoordinated, clumsy movement. Often associated with disorders of the cerebellum.

100. **nystagmus:**   involuntary movements of the eyes, usu-ally rapid and jerky; seen often with cerebellar vestib-ular disorders.

101. **dysarthria:**   difficulty in speaking clearly or articulat-ing. Caused by weakness or poor control of muscles of mouth such as the lips, tongue, and palate.

102. **vertigo:**   a sensation of spinning or a sensation that the world around you is spinning. Vertigo has many causes, including disorders of the middle or inner ear.

103. **dysphagia:**   difficulty in swallowing.

104. **quadriplegia:**   paralysis of all four limbs.

105. **locked-in syndrome:**   paralysis of the limbs and much of the head area creating an inability to speak even though the person is mentally intact; caused by local injury to part of the pons.

106. **focal:**   injuries to a localized area of a tissue or organ such as the brain.

107. **postconcussion syndrome:**   a group of symptoms occurring after mild head injury that may persist for days, weeks, or months. The symptoms may include physical and mental complaints which can interfere with life functions such as work, study, leisure pursuits, and sex.

108. **organic:**   pertaining to the organs of the body; physical. Also called "primary" in this book.

109. **functional:**   inorganic, showing no evidence of body abnormalities; psychological in origin. Also called "secondary" in this book.

110. **nerve root:**   radiculopathy: a disease or injury of a spinal nerve root. The root is a motor or sensory cable directing connections to and from peripheral nerves and one segment of spinal cord.

111. **nerve plexus:**   plexopathy: a disease or injury of one of the nerve plexuses: either the lumbosacral plexus or the brachial plexus. The brachial plexus forms nerves that serve the upper extremities. The lumbosacral plexus forms nerves serving the pelvic organs, including the sex organs and the lower limbs.

112. **peripheral nerve:**   the cable system conveying sensory, motor, or a mixture of both types of nerve fibers, to and from segments of the body and spinal cord.

Most peripheral nerves carry a mixture of sensory and motor fibers as well as autonomic nerve fibers. The sensory fibers come from skin and deep tissue receptors and convey information to the spinal cord, thalamus, and the sensory strip of the brain. The motor fibers connect to muscle groups and cause them to contract. The autonomic fibers connect to glands, blood vessels, and organ smooth muscles to control nonwilled activities.

**113.** *hydrocephalus:* an excessive amount of cerebral fluid in the brain causing expansion of the ventricles and possible injury to the brain. Sometimes seen as a complication of brain injury.

**114.** *dyspareunia:* painful intercourse in either sex. Causes may be physical or psychological.

**115.** *premature ejaculation:* ejaculation of sperm early or at the beginning of a sexual act. It usually leaves the partner unsatisfied and the man frustrated. The cause is functional.

**116.** *vaginismus:* often painful tightening of the vagina due to spasm of muscles surrounding, or adjacent to, the vagina. Penetration by the penis may be difficult or impossible.

**117.** *aphonia:* inability to utter sounds.

**118.** *lumbosacral plexus:* a grouping and combination of spinal nerve roots that form individual peripheral nerves. They are located within the pelvis and subject to injury with pelvic fractures. The nerves formed by the plexus serve the lower extremities and genitalia.

**119.** *neuropathy:* a disease or injury of a peripheral nerve or nerves.

**120.** *anticholinergic drugs:* drugs which antagonize the effects of acetylcholine, a neurotransmitter. Often prescribed for gastrointestinal disorders.

121. ***retrograde ejaculation:***   the ejection of seminal fluid backward into the bladder. This is usually due to a neurological disorder.

122. ***anorgasmia:***   consistent inability to experience a climax.

123. ***gynecological:***   relating to reproductive and urinary system function and disorders in women.

124. ***equilibrium:***   relating to, or a state of, balance.

125. ***external genitalia:***   the primary sex organs on the surface of the body. In the male, the penis and scrotum (sac containing the testes). In the female, the labia (lips), the clitoris, and the vaginal opening.

126. ***gingiva:***   the gums. Gingival hypertrophy is the overgrowth of gum tissue, a frequent complication of long-standing use of Dilantin, an antiseizure drug.

127. ***heterotopic bone:***   formation of bone in abnormal sites, usually in soft tissues adjacent to joints. Commonly seen in shoulders, elbows, hips, and knees.

128. ***lability:***   a brief display of emotion, most often laughing or crying with little or no provocation. Seen with brain injury or disease involving the cerebrum.

129. **AIDS:**   autoimmune disease syndrome caused by human immunodeficiency virus (HIV), and transmitted by infected blood. Therefore contaminated syringes and needles, as well as bisexual activities transmit AIDS.

130. ***sexual identity:***   the realization of one's gender. Developmentally, sexual identity normally occurs by 2½ to 3 years of age.

131. ***adaptive aids:***   devices to substitute for impaired function. For example, a reacher to compensate for limited arm reach or ability to bend over.

132. ***dildo:***   an external device for sexual stimulation, generally the shape and consistency of an erect penis.

133. *physical modalities*:    agents such as heat, cold, electricity, hydrotherapy, traction, stretching, massage, splinting, and bracing.

134. *biofeedback*:    the use of information derived from body processes to influence or control those processes. Example: the display of muscle activity on a screen with sound so that the person can learn to "turn off" the signals by relaxing the muscle on display.

135. *contracture*:    a fixed shortening of a soft tissue structure; limiting the full range of motion or inhibiting all motion of that structure.

136. *cognitive training*:    an educational training system usually directed by psychologists with particular skills and training in this field. Programs may utilize many methods including formal education, individualized computer programs, problem-solving training, daily living skills training, interpersonal and social skills training, preparation for vocational attainment training, and the like.

137. *augmentative communications devices*:    various methods of communication for individuals who are either without voice production, or whose speech and/or writing are severely impaired. The devices may be simple substitutions such as a chart of illustrations or involve sophisticated electronic systems of coded speech or printing.

138. *transitional living centers*:    programs for recovering persons in the community that stress education and training in skills of community living such as homemaking, transacting business, shopping, socializing, and so forth.

139. *day hospital programs*:    outpatient programs providing a diverse number of services to individuals who require intensive services without hospitalization. For rehabilitation programs, multiple therapies may be

provided up to 6 hours daily for as many as 5 days per week.

**140.** *independent living cooperatives*:    housing-living projects in which disabled persons may attain partial or total independence; projects in which self-governance and self-maintenance are core principles.

**141.** *behavior training centers*:    programs which focus on people with severe behavioral problems that require institutionalization. Psychological, psychiatric, and educational-training techniques are frequently employed together over periods of months.

**142.** *muscle transfer*:    the cutting of the tendinous end of muscle and inserting that end at a new site so that the action of the muscle is changed.

**143.** *intrathecal Baclofen*:    the administration of the anti-spasticity drug Baclofen into the spinal canal from the surgically placed pump. Used in cases of severe spasticity.

**144.** *anesthetic block*:    injection of local anesthetic drug into a part of the nervous system in order to temporarily interrupt the function of that part of the system; often used in the management of pain.

**145.** *sympathectomy*:    surgical interruption of a part of the sympathetic nervous system, such as the treatment for causalgia.

**146.** *sympathetic nervous system*:    that part of the autonomic nervous system producing blood vessel constriction, pupil dilation, thick scanty saliva, rapid heart rate, and decreased digestive activity. These "fight or flight" reactions are regulated through the release of the neurotransmitter noradrenalin.

**147.** *autonomic nervous system*:    the part of the nervous system controlling involuntary bodily functions, especially those of glands, smooth muscle, heart muscle, and adrenal gland. It is divided into the sympathetic and parasympathetic nervous systems.

148. *joint fusion:*    the locking of a joint so that there is no movement. It can happen as the result of disease, prolonged immobility, or as a surgical treatment.

149. *vascular:*    pertaining to blood vessels; peripheral vascular relates to the vessels in the limbs.

150. *gay:*    a male homosexual.

151. *lesbian:*    a female homosexual.

152. *contraception:*    any    reversible    or    "permanent" method of birth control. The "permanent" surgical division of the fallopian tubes (woman) or vas deferens (man) may occasionally be reconstructed successfully.

153. *intrauterine device:*    a contraceptive device that is medically inserted into the uterine cavity.

154. *cervical cap:*    a contraceptive device that fits closely over the uterine cervix. It is rarely used today.

155. *chlamydial infections:*    sexually transmitted infections caused by a viruslike microscopic organism. Sites of infection include the lower urinary tract, vagina, and female pelvic organs of reproduction. The infections are curable with oral antibiotics.

156. *herpes of the genital organs:*    sexually transmitted infection caused by a virus closely related to the one producing the common "cold" or "fever" sore. Sites of infection include the external genitalia, vagina, and uterine cervix. Controllable with an antiviral drug but tends to recur.

157. *venereal warts:*    sexually transmitted infection caused by a wart-virus. Warts appear on the external genitalia, vagina, and uterine cervix. Curable with local application of chemicals or liquid nitrogen.

158. *trichomonas infections:*    sexually transmitted infections caused by a parasite. Sites of infection include

lower urinary tract, vagina, and uterine cervix. Curable with an oral medicine.

## TERMS DEFINED IN ALPHABETICAL ORDER

# INDEX

A page number followed by a "t" indicates a table; a page number followed by an "f" represents a figure.